Introduction to a Quest for a New Star Wisdom– Astrosophy

By
Hazel Straker

An Introduction to the Quest for a New Star Wisdom -
Astrosophy

© Hazel Sraker

ISBN 0-9524403-7-7

Published by:
Anastasi Ltd., The Throne, Weobley Herefordshire HR4 8SW.

Typeset in Minion by: Anastasi Ltd.

Printed and Bound in Great Britain by
Biddles Ltd.
Guildford and King's Lynn.

Cover by: Anastasi Ltd. Design Studio
Cover painting: © Hazel Sraker 2000

Contents

An Introduction to the Quest for a New Star Wisdom - Astrosophy

The quest for a New Star Wisdom, which has become known as Astrosophy, is a comparatively new science brought to birth in 1924 by Dr. Elizabeth Vreede. At that time she was given the task by Dr. Rudolf Steiner of creating a Mathematical-Astronomical Section within the spiritual scientific work arising at the Goetheanum in Switzerland.

This series of articles came into being through various requests over the last 12 years. Besides the fundamental suggestions of Dr. Steiner and the further working of Dr. Vreede the writer is especially indebted to Willi 0. Sucher who took up this particular aspect of Dr. Vreede's work and devoted the last 57 years of his life to developing it further. In most cases the original tense in which the article was written has been maintained. Dates should lead to clarification.

Contemplations on the Total Eclipse of the Sun in August 1999

On August the 9th, 1999, 65 of us from various places in Great Britain, the continent of Europe and USA. found our way to a Manor House near Slaughterbridge, Cornwall, in the south west of England. We came to celebrate the total Sun Eclipse on the 11th with a four day Astronomical Conference. The Manor House was near the legendary site of the last great battle of King Arthur with Mordred which cost him his life. We enjoyed talks, discussions and two concerts but of course the climax of it all was the day of the eclipse.

Not being quite in the total shadow area we drove about 10 miles south, most of us gathering on Bodmin Moor a large upland area of common grazing land with various little hills crowned with rocky outcrops. Parking the cars we climbed one of the small rocky knolls together with an increasing number of other people all with the same intent. The sky was partly clouded and the weather man held out little hope that we should be able to see what we had all come there for. However, soon after we arrived gaps in the cloud let us see the first ingress of the Moon in front of the Sun. The wind got up, gaining strength as we watched the increasing coverage of the Sun through cloud-veiled portals so that we did not need our special glasses. More and more people streamed up the hill, whole families, also with their dogs, as the wind grew colder and stronger and the clouds thicker.

After sighting the last little sliver of the Sun the clouds completely veiled our sight of the celestial drama but what unfolded on Earth and in the realm of the clouds was an unforgettable experience of a lifetime. The clouds to the west grew heavier and darker, forming great drop-like areas of darkness. The light grew dimmer and dimmer until the street lights appeared in the distance. All around were manifold flashes of light which turned out to be the many cameras trying to record the event. Whereas to the east and around most of the horizon it was still much lighter, appearing for a time with sunset/sunrise hue. An awe-inspiring cloud of darkness rushed towards us like a great black Being. Awe-inspiring but not menacing. The darkness rose to its climax and there was a burst of applause from the people gathered around; then it was over with the new born light dispelling the darkness. The Sun remained totally hidden behind dark clouds as for a time the people remained exchanging their experiences which seemed to be dominated by an overwhelming feeling of awe at the magnitude of the cosmic spectacle, so brief but so magnificent.

It had grown so cold that we were glad to make our way back to the cars and have something to eat and drink before returning to our Manor House. It was all so unexpectedly magnificent and overwhelming that I was glad of a brief sleep before we gathered to share our experiences. Although I had longed to see the corona and diamond ring, that our attention had been directed more eathwards turned out to be a blessing, giving a living experience of the Mystery of Golgotha - a Death and Resurrection in our Age. It was wonderful to share this with all those fellow human beings; a common experience of the majesty of the Divine World.

Did the reverence of the countless human beings turned towards the dark shadow being transform his possibly menacing appearance into an awe-inspiring challenge? Can we now move towards a Whitsun experience as we approach the celestial events of the coming year?

Hazel Straker

WHY ASTROSOPHY?

There are certain sentences in Rudolf Steiner's lectures and written work which challenge us each individually and remain to be pondered over, perhaps for a life-time. For me one such sentence is:

> If the correlation between the earth and the extra-terrestrial world, that is the cosmic world, is not comprehended again on a level of spiritual understanding, then the Mystery of Golgotha cannot live on, cannot survive into the future.[1]

Rudolf Steiner has made it abundantly clear that the central event of the seven great stages of evolution was the deed of Christ on Golgotha and therefore that the understanding of this forms the heart of spiritual science, Anthropos-Sophia, the wisdom of the human being. This wisdom obviously contains the knowledge of the cosmic origin of humankind. We know how we had to leave our cosmic home for a time to learn to understand the mission of humanity through dwelling on the earth. The seed for the reunion of heaven and earth was laid by the Christ during that process which was visible on earth during the three years when Christ dwelt in the body of Jesus. In the last of three lectures which Rudolf Steiner reworked for the booklet *The Spiritual Guidance of Mankind*[2] he states: 'Now spiritual science must recognise in Christ not merely an earthly but also a cosmic being.' And further on: 'The Christ stood always under the influence of the entire cosmos–He made no step without this working of the cosmic forces into and in Him.' Still further on: 'The forces active within Him, however, were the cosmic forces coming from the sun and stars; and these directed His body. And it was always in accordance with the collective being of the whole universe, with whom the earth is in harmony, that all which the Christ Jesus did took place.'

Turning to two other references concerning the stars we hear: 'As we look at the outer, physical radiance of the planets, we know that each of these heavenly bodies is but the sign that in that direction where we behold it there is a colony of spiritual beings in the cosmos.'[3] And:

'Inasmuch as we contemplate the world of the stars, we contemplate the bodies of the Gods and finally of the Divine in general.'[4]

From this we can get the picture of Christ Jesus walking on the earth and around Him, in the heavens, the stars and their gestures manifesting the totality of the world of spirit beings - all the ranks of the hierarchies which constitute the greater being of Christ. Then, obviously, all that He does on earth would be in harmony with His whole being, not dominated by but working in harmony with those spiritual beings.

> Now we see the stars as expressions of something real, I compared their action to a gentle caressing. The spirit-selfhood that is behind them is indeed the being that caresses lovingly, only in this case it is not a single being but the whole world of the hierarchies.[5]

In the Gospel of St John, Christ Jesus says to His disciples immediately after the washing of their feet: 'Most assuredly, I say to you, he who believes in me, the works that I do he will do also; and greater works than these will he do, because I go to my Father.'[6] If we take this seriously we can come to the thought that this relationship of Christ Jesus to the starry worlds during the three years he was on earth was a deed initiating the possibility for all mankind to do the same: to progress from being a receiver, guided by the spiritual beings, to becoming a giver, offering up the fruits of our experience on earth. For Christ did not only live in harmony with those beings in the cosmic worlds but infused the seeds for a new cosmos, which can only come about through the participation of human beings out of a free, conscious decision.

But why must the visible stars come into this? Can it not be worked at solely in the realm of thought? In the Letter to Members with the title 'The Human Future and Michael's Activity' Rudolf Steiner writes:

> Michael counts it as his deepest satisfaction that *through the agency of man* he has succeeded in keeping the starry world directly united with the divine-spiritual in the following way: When man has lived out his life between death and rebirth and is beginning his descent to a new earth existence, he *seeks*, on his way down, to establish harmony between the movements of the stars and his own life on earth. Unless man sought it, this harmony - which had previously been a matter of course… would not today exist in movements of the stars that have become the mere *effect* of previous activity… It is *Michael's deed* that this can be, and this deed causes him such deep satisfaction as to find in it part of his life-element, his life-energy, his sunlike life will.[7]

Rudolf Steiner goes on to say that the world man experiences around him during his life between birth and death is now even further removed from the Divine Spirit; it is no longer even the workings of Divine Spirit but its after-effects, what 'might be called wrought work'. Do the visible stars not belong to this 'wrought work'? This visible world around us only exists through the sacrifice of spiritual beings who have been held back in their evolution to bring about an environment to which man can 'bring his own being as it has developed in the present epoch'.[8] Thus we are privileged to have the task of participating in the transformation, transubstantiation of the cosmos, including our earth, so that: 'It is no longer the same being once present as the cosmos that will receive its illumination from humanity. As the divine-spiritual passes through humanness, it will experience a quality of being not previously manifested.'[9]

Some readers will be familiar with the lecture Rudolf Steiner gave on New Year's Eve 1922-3 at the First Goetheanum, one hour before the fire was discovered. In it we are called upon to re-enliven the solid and fluid elements within and around us by raising into our consciousness their connection with the realm of the resting stars, the zodiac, and what he calls the deeds of the stars, the movements of the planets, and thereby transforming them through the power of our will and feeling. Thus we can raise our 'relationship to the world from knowledge into cosmic ritual, which is needed if anthroposophy is to fulfil its mission in the world.'[10]

All this would help to form a background out of which to start a quest for a new star wisdom, first becoming acquainted with the rhythms and gestures of the starry world and then their relationship to the earthly world and the being of man. It is this latter realm of research which raises so many misgivings. This matter is discussed in Rudolf Steiner's lecture on *Karmic Relationships* of 18 September 1924.[11] He describes how our soul, after death, lives and moves among the stars, which are colonies of spiritual beings. Here, together with other human souls we prepare for a new birth. Rudolf Steiner continues:

> To understand karma, therefore, we must return once more to a wisdom of the stars. We must discover spiritually the paths of the human being between death and a new birth in connection with the beings of the stars. Now until the beginning of the age of Michael there were the greatest difficulties for people of the modern age to approach a real wisdom of the stars. And anthroposophy, having nevertheless found its way to such a wisdom, must be deeply thankful for the fact that the dominion of Michael really did enter the life of human beings on earth with the last third of the 19th century. For among many things that we owe to the dominion of Michael there is this too: we have gained once more unhindered access to discover what must be investigated in the worlds of the stars if we would understand karma and the forming of karma in the sphere of humanity. [12]

Rudolf Steiner then points to great difficulties which are to be encountered in karmic research and how certain souls can feel apprehensive in approaching a science of the stars, also of karma, through their having had unfortunate experiences with the unchristian cosmology of the Middle Ages, a wisdom of the stars 'unrighteously applied'. He cites the background of the figure of Strader in his Mystery Plays. However, he says that these difficulties can be overcome if one enlists the help of Michael and that it is necessary to do this 'in order that at length a number of human beings, united karmically in the community of Michael, can learn to know the things of karma'.[13] It is here that I believe we so badly need each other, for by sharing our research experiences before sending them out into the world we can help each other not to fall into the many possibilities of error.

I should like to add one other thought, concerning the unchristian cosmology of the Middle Ages. In ancient times, when our consciousness was more orientated to the cosmos than to the realm of earth, star wisdom was a royal wisdom only available to the leaders of mankind. Evolution moved on to the turning-point of time, when the three kings appeared as the last outer manifestation of carriers of that royal star wisdom. They were representatives of a stream of wisdom guarded in the mystery schools since the time of the second post-Atlantean Cultural epoch, the Persian.

Through it they were able to know the time of the rebirth of their great leader Zar-athustra, the child who was to play a vital part in forming the vessel to receive the Christ 30 years later. Knowledge of the spiritual world faded and the surface knowledge of the stars became astrology. Although some aspects were preserved in their purity much became distorted owing to lack of real understanding. By working out of the Michael-Christ impulse, can we fulfil what Rudolf Steiner describes as his deep inner experience?

> It became clearer and clearer to me - as the outcome of many years of research - that in our epoch there is really something like a resurrection of the astrology of the third epoch, but permeated now with the Christ impulse.[14]

The changing relationship between human beings and the stars is summed up in a verse Rudolf Steiner composed at the time he gave the lectures on *The Spiritual Communion of Mankind* held over Christmas 1922. In the verse Rudolf Steiner calls to our highest principle, spirit man; however, he speaks of a process already initiated. The future must always be prepared. The preparation for the future is now.

The Stars once spoke to Man
It is World-destiny
That they are silent now
To be aware of that silence
Can become pain for earthly
Man.

But in the deepening silence
There grows and ripens
What Man speaks to the Stars
To be aware of the speaking
Can become strength for Spirit-
Man.[15]

NOTES
1 *Blätter fr Anthroposophie, Vol.4 No.6* .
2 Rudolf Steiner, *The Spiritual Guidance of Mankind*, lecture of 8 June 1911.
3 Rudolf Steiner, *Karmic Relationships*, Vol. II, Lecture XXIV, 29 May 1924.
4 Rudolf Steiner, *The Spiritual Beings in the Heavenly Bodies*, Lecture 5, 7 April 1912.
5 Rudolf Steiner, *The Festivals and their Meaning*, Vol. 3, Ascension and Pentecost, Lecture 6, 4 June 1924.
6 John: 14;12.
7 Rudolf Steiner, *The Michael Mystery*, 'The Human Future and Michael's Activity', letter of 2 November 1924 (trans. Marjorie Spock).
8 Ibid.
9 Ibid.
10 Rudolf Steiner *The Spiritual Communion of Mankind*, Lecture 5, 31 December 1922
11 Rudolf Steiner *Karmic Relationships*, Vol IV, Lecture VII, 18 September 1924.
12 Ibid.
13 Ibid.
14 Rudolf Steiner *Christ and the Spiritual World and the Search for the Holy Grail*, Lecture 5, 1 January 1914.
15 Verse given to Marie Steiner, 25 December 1922, in *Verses and Meditations*.

SIGNS AND CONSTELLATIONS

How often one hears someone asserting 'I am a Virgo' or 'I am a Pisces' or any other of the twelve zodiac signs! But how many can tell you on what that assertion is based? They might perhaps know that it has to do with certain characteristics they may have and with what time of the year they were born, but even if one knows that, like our watch-time and our calendars, it is based on the rhythms of the Sun, there is still a further complication. The yearly calendar is computed from the movement of the Sun in front of the twelve constellations of the zodiac. However, someone born on say, February 11, knows his birth sign is Aquarius, but astronomers know the stars behind the Sun are those of Capricorn. What is this contradiction? The twelve visible constellations of the zodiac are of irregular size and shape: some - like the Lion or the Virgin are large and bright, others, like the Crab, are small and faint. These visible constellations are what astronomers describe and use, and they are always related to the visible stars.

Observation of the sun shows that besides the daily east-west movement of the Sun, he also moves in a circle from west to east each year, passing in front of the twelve groups of stars forming the zodiac. The background stars are not visible in the time that the Sun is in that constellation but they can be deduced mathematically. Two or three centuries before Christ the Sun's annual path, or *ecliptic*, was divided into twelve equal divisions which were given the same names as the visible constellations. The starting point for that circle was taken from where the Sun is at the time of the vernal equinox (northern hemisphere). This is one of the two points where the Sun's path, the ecliptic, crosses the extended equator of the Earth, the celestial equator. These two circles are tilted at 23½ because the axis of the Earth is tilted to that of the Sun's path. We experience this astronomical fact in the changing length of day and night in the course of the year, in the changing height of the noonday sun which brings about the seasons. When the Sun passes one of the two equinox points (in March and September) day and night are of equal length all over the globe, and the Sun rises due east and sets due west. Between these two points lie those of the solstices, where in the northern hemisphere in June the longest day is experienced and in December the shortest, with the opposite occurring in the southern regions.

There is a reality in the Sun's yearly course, and this is directly reflected in the different seasonal phenomena experienced simultaneously over the Earth, rhythmically during the course of the year. This is something which has been happening through the ages, although the character of the seasons may have changed. It has always been possible to take as a starting point the Sun's position when moving through the equinox, and astronomers measure the positions of the planets from this point. The twelve equal divisions of the sun's yearly path are called the signs of the zodiac and take their starting point at the spring equinox in March Fig.1.

Observation over long periods of time shows a further complication. The vernal equinox does not remain in the same place against the background of the Sun, but moves slowly from east to west (about 1 every 70 years), taking nearly 26,000 years to move through the circle of the zodiac.

If we could see the stars behind the Sun when he now moves through that vernal point (or spring equinox) into the sign of Aries, we would find the stars of the constellation of Pisces. But going back to around the time of Christ, the Sun's vernal point would have appeared before the gap between the group of stars forming the Ram and those of the constellation of the Fishes. Since that time, the Sun has appeared –at the spring vernal equinox– progressively deeper into the Fishes, and can now be 'seen' under the tail of the western fish. Likewise, the September equinox point and the solstices change their relationship to the visible star world.

This 'great year' is also known as the Platonic Year, although it seems to have been discovered by the Greek astronomer Hipparchus (about 190-120 BC) after the lifetime of Plato. Hipparchus became aware of this rhythm through patient and very exact observation, the results of which he then compared with those of earlier astronomers. It marks out the ages, each comprising about 2160 years, and manifests through history in the rise and fall of different periods of culture. Most of us have heard of the present Age of Pisces, and a short time ago there was much talk that we were entering the Age of Aquarius. There are different opinions, many fully justified, as to where the exact divisions between the constellations fall, and obviously transition periods also come into consideration.

Readers who have had the patience and perseverance to follow through this attempt to describe some of the astronomical laws behind the observable phenomena may nevertheless be wondering what all this has to do with each one of us. I would like to suggest the thought that the seemingly dry facts of astronomical laws are 'open secrets' and can become the doors or windows to greater spiritual

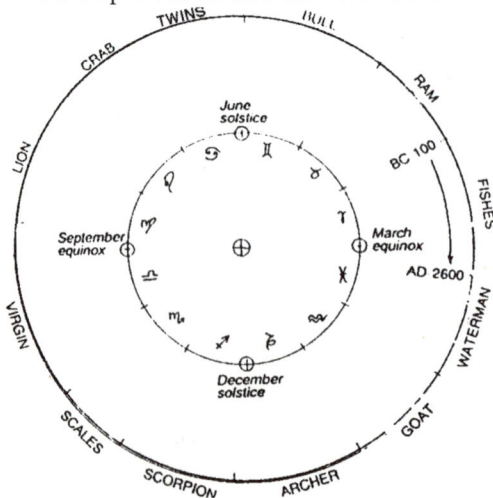

Fig. 1 – The inner circle represents the sun's yearly path (ecliptic) around the Earth, divided into twelve equal signs. The arrow shows the changing relationship of the March equinox point, the sun entering the sign of the Ram (♈), to the outer circle of the visible constellations.

truths of which we are an integral part. We have already suggested that the equinox points indicate a close relationship between the sphere of our Earth and that of the Sun. Could they be gateways to the universe of the greater Sun? Through the different Ages this 'gateway' would be open for inspiration coming from the twelve regions of this greater Sun. Could this not be taken up by individuals and peoples, thus bringing about the evolution of consciousness within humanity? Let us look at how that would have been at the time of Christ.

The experience of the Resurrection as described in the Gospels tells of events in the early morning of the first day of the week, Sunday. The Full Moon had taken place on Friday at the time of the Crucifixion. By tradition, verified recently by research, the first Good Friday took place on April 3, about 10 days after the Sun had passed the spring vernal point (these are the three 'pointers' by which we know when Easter should fall in any given year). So, on that first Easter Sunday the Sun rose in the sign of the Ram, the first division of the ecliptic, and also before the stars of the constellation of the Ram. There was harmony between signs and constellations when the mighty impulse brought by the Christ Being from his dwelling place in the Greater Sun streamed into the Earth through the gateway of the Sun.

Soon after that, this Sun gate opened towards the stars of the Fishes – a new Age had been inaugurated, signified by the early Christians who used the symbol of the Fishes for the Christ. But the Earth with her girdle of the ecliptic has since then been turning away from a direct connection with the extra-solar world which, according to present reckoning, will not take this form again in the sense meant here for nearly 26,000 years.

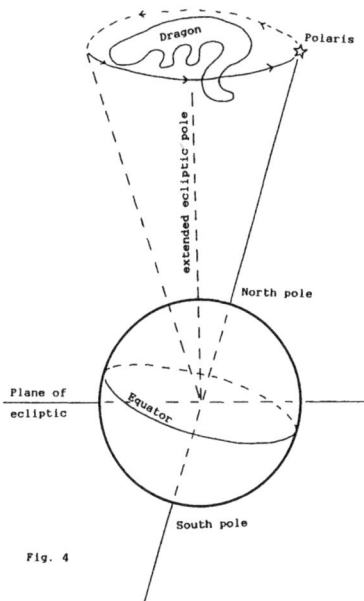

Fig. 2 – Circle traced on the heavens by the extended pole of the Earth through its 'wobble' around the extended ecliptic pole over 26,000 years.

A further astronomical law explains that this is brought about by the 'wobble' of the pole of our Earth. This will not always point to the North Star as at present, but will trace a circle in the heavens round the constellation of the Dragon who holds the ecliptic pole, returning to Polaris again in about 26,000 years and bringing about the so-called precession of the vernal equinox point Fig. 2 (see also pages 27-28). Could we entertain the thought that when signs and constellations again coincide we could have so worked with the Christ impulse that we humankind could shine something new into the realm of the greater Sun?

THE DANCE OF THE STARS FROM THE VIEWPOINT OF THE EARTH - 1.

Working on the land we have around us the kingdoms of nature, plants, trees and animals, and in getting to know them we become aware of a whole world of rhythms out of which they live and grow. Our life too is based on rhythms but how often do we raise our thoughts to the realm from which the rhythms come? For this we need to look out beyond the horizon of our earth to the dance of the stars as we experience them around us. Because we are here concerning ourselves with life on earth we shall take the geocentric or earth-centred view of the starry world and not the more general view which considers the Sun as the centre of movement. There is no contradiction between these two viewpoints, neither is right nor wrong. How different we each look from the front or from the back, not to mention the two sides! We know we need all these views to gain a total picture of the human form. Would not the greater world also need to be viewed from more than one viewpoint to gain a more comprehensive understanding of it? For our direct experience the movement of the Sun around us gives us the basis for our daily life. Have you ever thought how it would be if one morning the Sun would not rise, even behind the clouds? Who marks out for us our calendar year? The Sun. Who marks out the Ages which form the great Platonic year? Again it is the Sun. For our year we follow the Sun's movement before twelve constellations of the Zodiac; for the Platonic year it is the slow procession of the vernal point northern hemisphere, which the Sun crosses each year on 20th or 21st of March.

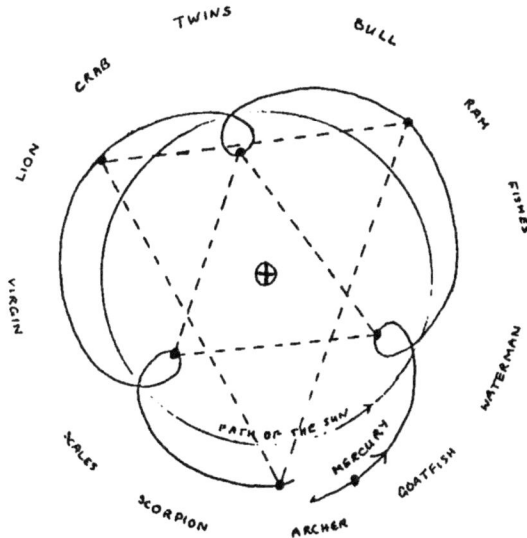

Fig.3–

Mercury's path through 1987

On earth we swim within the encompassing cloak of the fixed star heavens, those groups of stars who appear to remain in the same relationship to each other for long periods of time, shining with their own light like our Sun. As a great highway these are the twelve groups known as the Zodiac which is always encircling us; before these twelve we observe the planets or moving stars performing a manifold, rhythmic dance which brings them in ever changing relationships to each other and to the stars of the Zodiac. The planets, who form the solar system or Sun family (to which our earth also belongs) take their light from the Sun and shine it back. The Sun belongs to both the fixed star world and to that of the planets.

We can all become aware of the Sun's rhythms fairly easily, but what of the other planets? Can we in any way 'observe' the rest of that great cosmic dance with its myriad patterns and rhythms? Astronomically we can make a picture of that encompassing cloak of rhythms constantly being woven around us which can fill us with such awe and wonder. Mercury so loves the Sun that he cannot bear to be too far from him and so circles the Sun in his yearly path, tracing out the pattern of a six-pointed star around us on earth. Venus moves more slowly but also dances around the Sun, taking eight years to indicate a double five-pointed star around us. Mars moves much more slowly and does not mind getting opposite the Sun in the Zodiac when he comes close to greet us one year, the following year being overtaken by the Sun while he is moving far beyond him from our point of view. He takes sixteen years to weave a flower or star which has eight large petals or points and eight smaller ones Fig. 5. Jupiter and Saturn move still more slowly, always beyond the Sun's path, weaving a

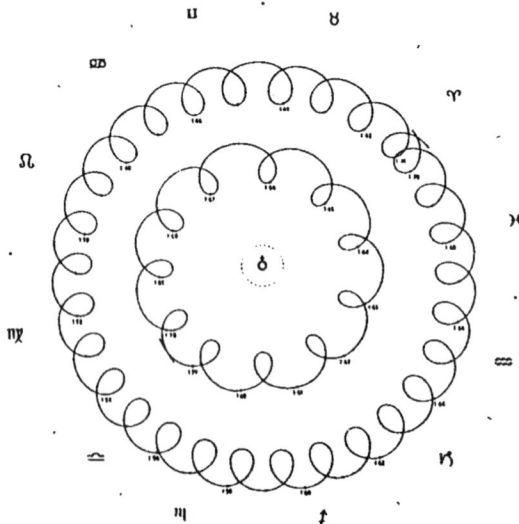

Fig.4 –

Geocentric paths of Saturn (1940 – 1970)
and Jupiter (1959 – 1970)

lace-like pattern as they nod in towards the earth or move further out each year, taking almost 12 and 30 years to dance before all twelve constellations of the Zodiac. When any planets come close to the Sun we are not able to see them as they are outshone by it but from the times when we can observe them in the twilight or night time we can begin to become aware of the wonder of this cosmic geometry. In this article it is only possible to give a brief indication of some of the movements and gestures within this great dance. Later we hope to be able to build up a fuller picture also in relationship to current events in the starry world.

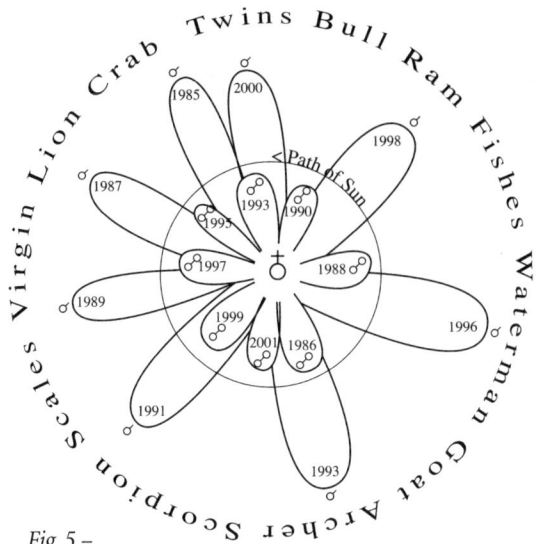

Fig. 5 –
The 16 petalled flower Mars and the Sun weave around us from 1985 to 2001 ♂ Conjunction with the Sun, ♂° Opposition to the Sun.

Many people during the month of August have become aware of special events between the planets which they felt called on mankind to seek ways of establishing a new harmonious relationship between human beings on earth and the extraterrestial world of the stars. The actual phenomena in the sky were remarkable and possibly unique. Between August 20 and 25 1987, five planets had meetings with each other within a few degrees of the circle of the Zodiac. As one of them was the Sun this was not visible with the naked eye so we need to exercise our power of imagination to form a picture. Let us go back to August 24 and journey out from the earth in ever widening spirals through the spheres marked by the planets. Firstly we would have come to the Moon, New Moon, and then to the Sun. Further out beyond the Sun we would have found the planets Mercury, Venus, and Mars. Continuing out to the realm of the fixed stars, behind that great line up was Regulus, the heart of the lion, the brightest star in the constellation of Leo. Saturn and Uranus are moving through the tail end of the constellation of Scorpion with Neptune nearby having entered the area of the Archer or Sagittarius. Jupiter has just moved into the region of the Ram or Aries. Joining in what has been termed the great Harmonic Convergence these four planets formed 130 anglular relationships to the other five during the month of August. Thus a great triangle was written in the sky around us by these nine planets. Not to be left out, the planet Pluto, the last to be counted as a member of the Sun family, formed quintile or 72 relationships with his fellow planets gathered before the Lion, between August 15 and 24. Pluto is moving between the Virgin and the Scales. What a grand Cosmic Imagination, and all centered in the Heart of the Lion, recounted in Mythology as the area from which the Sun was born. Jupiter has been clearly visible during these events. He will move back before the Fishes, increasing in brilliance until mid-October when he rises at sunset. From the end of September Venus will appear as evening star in the west, after sunset.

But what about the relationship of the stars to our earth? Can we experience anything of this as we work on the land? In earlier times this connection was an obvious fact to farmers and gardeners but today we must seek it out in ways acceptable to the present stage of consciousness which demands a scientific approach. Correlations have already been established in many realms but much more research is needed. To mention a few examples of work already carried out: Homoeopathic medicines and plant juices can be preserved for many years by exposing them to the rising and setting sun for a definite period of time. The growth patterns of plants, for instance, how the leaves are arranged around the stem, flower and seed patterns,

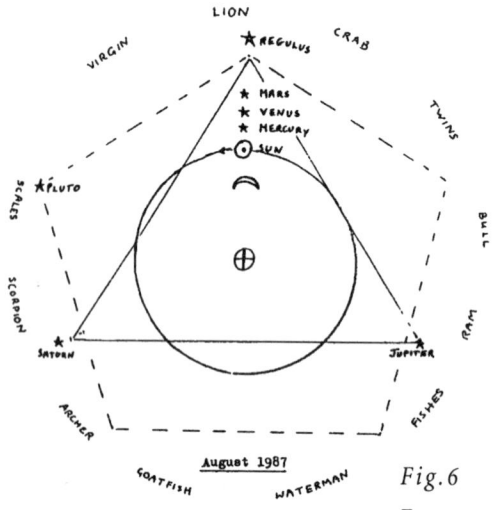

Fig. 6

can be found to follow the same geometric laws as the dance of the planets. Tree buds, which appear to sleep through the winter, have a subtle breathing movement in harmony with the various planetary relationships to each other. Plants and trees have been observed to grow more healthily when cared for in harmony with certain happenings in the starry world.

There is already enough evidence to suggest a need for the plants and animals to grow and live together with that which flows and weaves from the greater universe around us, manifest in the 'Dance of the Stars'. Does this not present us with a great challenge? To become ever more awake to and aware of the rhythms of the starry world and then to seek a deeper understanding. Only then can we become true healers of our earth and the kingdoms of nature.

THE DANCE OF THE STARS FROM THE VIEWPOINT OF THE EARTH 2.

In the last chapter we gave a few brief glimpses of some of the manifold starry gestures and now we shall start to build up a more detailed picture. Let us start out from wherever we are standing on the earth. We have around us the points of the compass, east, west, south and north. Looking east beyond the horizon of our earth the main event we observe is the rising of the Sun to start the hours of daylight. At times during the day we might also see the Moon rising. If we observe carefully after dark we shall see the various groups of so-called fixed stars coming up over the horizon one after the other during the whole night. These groups are formed by different numbers of stars who bear a definite or 'fixed' relationship to each other over long periods of time. This term is not quite correct as nothing in the universe is fixed; they do change the shape of their patterns over very long periods of time, but this is scarcely discernible during our individual lifetime. Another characteristic of them is that they have their own light, like our Sun, and appear to twinkle in the night sky. Patient observation through the year at the same time daily would reveal a series of different groups of stars appearing which would repeat itself in a yearly rhythm. Furthermore, watching the sweep of the horizon from the north east to the south east over the year one would notice that each specific group always appears at the same compass point and at the same time of the year. Thus when we become familiar with some of the constellations of stars we can know at which time of the year they would be visible in the evening sky towards the east. There is a legend from before the time of Christ of a watchman delegated to watch for an expected special star event by his master, one of the three kings or magi. It tells how during the long lonely nights he was cheered by greeting each group of stars as they rose like long lost friends.

Turning our gaze towards the western horizon we observe the opposite phenomena; the Sun and all the other stars we have watched rising in the east now vanish from our sight below the rim of the earth. They have the same relationship to the western point as they had to the east on rising. Within a certain area of the east and west points this rising and setting is a common experience from all places on earth. However, when we turn south and north we find counter pictures as in a mirror. Looking south in the northern hemisphere the stars move in rising curves from the east, culminating or reaching their highest position due south, and then continue in a falling curve to their setting in the west. In the southern hemisphere we must look north to see the culmination point in the east-west curving motion of the stars. The star patterns will also appear 'upside down' for those familiar with how they appear in the northern hemisphere, their movement from our right to our left, anti-clockwise, and the dimensions of their arcs opposite. We attempt to picture this in Figs. 7 and 10 with the star group of Orion, Sirius in the Great Dog, Castor and Pollux in the Twins and Capella in Auriga.

Looking north from the northern hemisphere we can observe the one star which, in our time, does not move, the Pole Star, Stella Polaris or Stella Maris, in the tail of the Little Bear. At all times of the day and night this star remains in the sky directly above the north point on the horizon, higher or lower according to the latitude from which it is viewed. It is the hub of the whole cloak of the starry heavens and those groups of stars nearby revolve round it in an anti-clockwise direction, never setting for places northward from near the equator. The seven stars in the Great Bear forming the Plough or Arthur's Wain, with its two pointer stars directing our gaze to Polaris, are the best known circumpolar group. At the north pole Polaris is directly above but lying on the horizon when viewed from the equator. If we imagine a line from the Pole Star down through the axis of the earth we would then come to a place in the heavens above the South Pole. Looking from the southern hemisphere southwards there is no

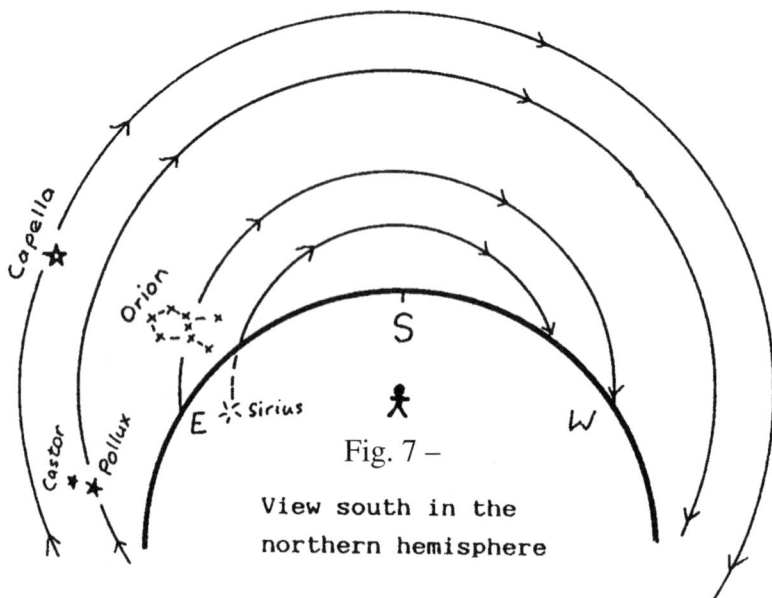

Fig. 7 –

View south in the
northern hemisphere

star marking this point in the heavens but nearby is the beautiful constellation of the Southern Cross which is as familiar to those living in the southern regions as the Plough is to those living north of the equator. The Southern Cross circles around the southern celestial pole but as we look south with the east on our left and west on our right the motion is clockwise. These two contrasting views are portrayed diagrammatically in Figs. 8 and 9.

It has seemed necessary to point out at least the main features of this world-wide

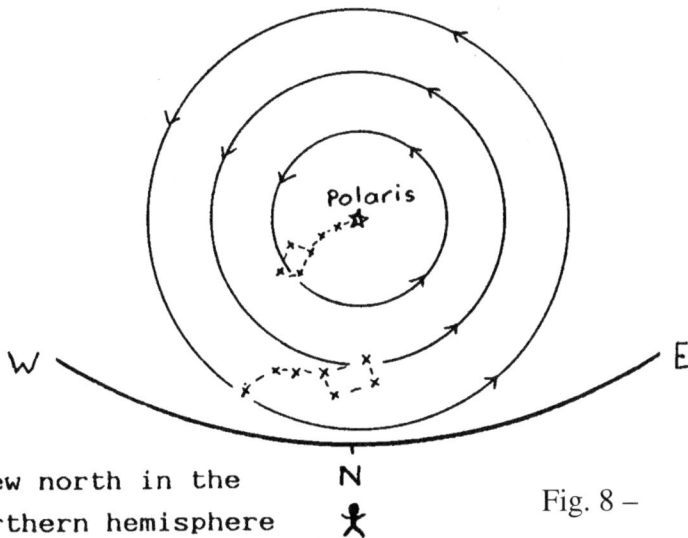

View north in the
northern hemisphere

N

Fig. 8 –

viewing of the heavens in order firstly to become aware of the many viewpoints which exist and to bring in all our readers wherever they may live on our planet earth. Those wishing to understand these phenomena more deeply are recommended to study *'Movements and Rhythms of the Stars'* by Joachim Schultz. This is a book for 'simple folk' like us as well as for those more versed in these happenings!

And now, hoping that readers still have two feet firmly on earth we will go on, with this background, to look at a part of the starry heavens common to all. In contrast to the regularly appearing groups of fixed stars there is the family of planets or wandering stars. As seen from the earth, there are seven visible wandering stars of which the Sun is one. However, unlike the Sun the other planets do not have their own light but reflect that of the Sun and shine with a steady light, each having their own quality and brilliance. They move in the space between us and the fixed star world marking out spheres of activity with which we and our planet earth are intimately connected. To the so-called classical planets whose rhythms have been noted through the ages, Moon, Mercury, Venus, Sun, Mars, Jupiter and Saturn, have been added, during the last 200 years, the further-out trio, Uranus, Neptune and Pluto, whose movements can only be observed, partly, through very powerful telescopes. Our earth as planet has also her movements and rhythms but to consider these we would have to look from another viewpoint in the universe and we have now chosen in the first place to look out from the earth which most of us experience as a firm point on which to stand. The Moon as the most conspicuous planet[†] shows us that this family appears at constantly different times through the years and with varying groups of fixed stars behind them. Furthermore it can be noted that although the planets rise at constantly varying points on the horizon they can only ever be seen moving across twelve of the many

†*Though Regarded as a satellite, classically it's known as a planet.*

21

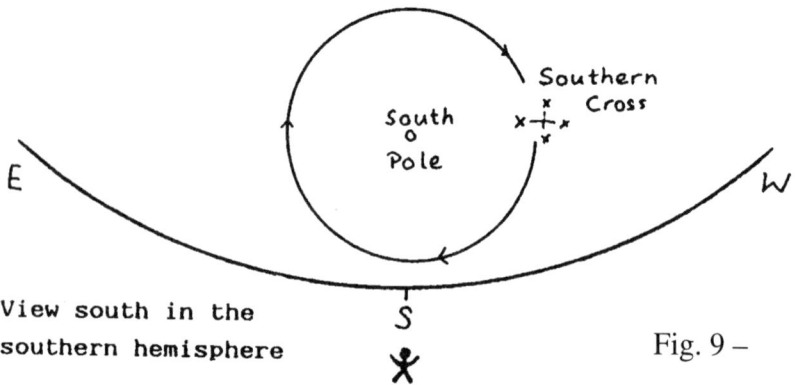

View south in the
southern hemisphere

Fig. 9 –

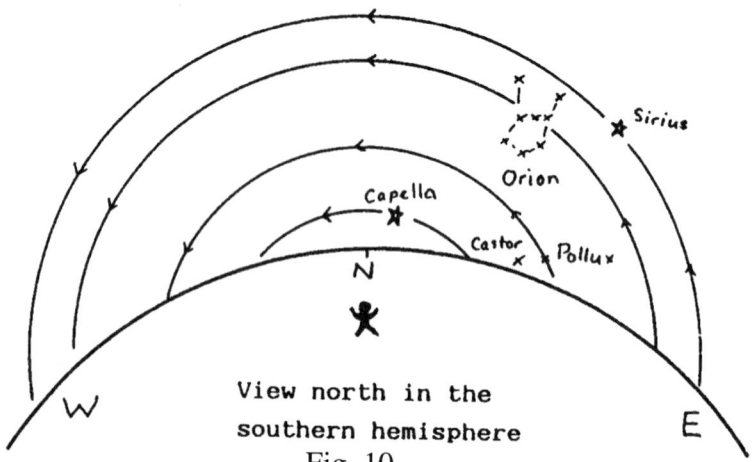

View north in the
southern hemisphere
Fig. 10 –

groups of fixed stars. These twelve are known as the constellations of the Zodiac, Ram or Aries, Bull or Taurus, Twins or Gemini, Crab or Cancer, Lion or Leo, Virgin or Virgo, Scales or Libra, Scorpion or Scorpio, Archer or Sagittarius, Goat or Capricorn, Waterman or Aquarius, Fishes or Pisces. Throughout the year they can be seen rising in that order, forming a circle around us with six above and six below the horizon at any one moment. These constellations and therefore also the planets are visible from all parts of the earth. We shall have to search in later chapters to see if we can find any qualitative relationship to these twelve different groups of stars as was experienced in past times and led to them being given the names which we still use but now rather more as a means of identification. First we shall lay some more groundwork of astronomical laws lying behind the various observable phenomena so that we can gradually begin to feel at home within this world of rhythm and life.

The daily movement of the Sun follows the circling of the whole starry sky each twenty four hours. As we said earlier he is always accompanied in the background by one of the twelve constellations of the Zodiac. The time measured by our clocks and watches is based on his crossing of the meridian at Greenwich. However, as this is slightly but rhythmically changing in the course of the year we have Greenwich Mean Time. Our timepieces are not living as is the living, breathing universe! Thus the Sun gives us the basis for the rhythm of our daily life in his east-west circling. If we could watch the stars in the constellation behind the Sun we would detect a slight change each day. Every day he falls behind the starry movements by about one degree. This means that he moves slowly backwards through each constellation passing from one to another in the reverse order from that of their daily appearance, from west to east. In the course of about 365 days he has traversed all twelve Zodiac groups, thus making our yearly calendar, which also has to be adjusted to the living rhythm of the Sun by the addition of one day every four years. Thus we have 29 days in February 1988 which is a leap year. There are four special points on the yearly path of the Sun, the solstices (21st or 22nd June and December) and the equinoxes (20th or 21st March and 22nd or 23rd September). The dates are deliberately given rather than the usual reference to the seasons, for with our global considerations we must always consider also the opposite season. The equinox times are marked world-wide by the

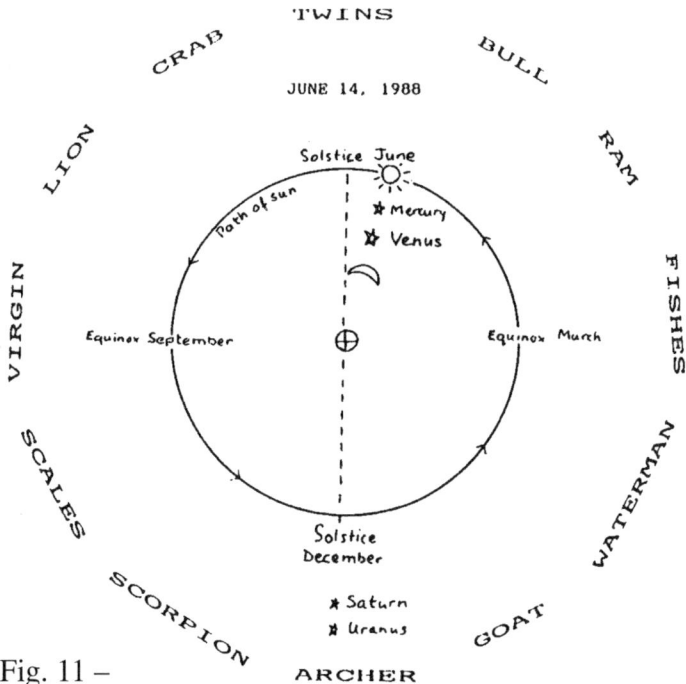

Fig. 11 –

23

equal length of night and day and the Sun rising due east and setting due west. The June solstice is marked by the longest day of the year in the northern hemisphere, summer, and the Sun rising furthest north of east, following its highest arc and setting north of west (the Sun just entering the Twins, see arc of Pollux in Fig. 7). It is winter in the southern hemisphere, the shortest day, with the Sun following a small arc from north east to north west (see Pollux in Fig. 10). We will go into this in more detail next time.

To conclude, let us look at some events during the second half of 1988 taking place near these four points. Early on June 13th the Sun will meet with Venus and Mercury within a timespan of four hours, just in the point of transition from Bull to Twins. The next day the Moon will pass all three to be New Moon at 9.14 GMT. Obviously this cannot be seen with our outer eyes but our wonderful power of imagination can evoke a picture of spiralling out through the Moon sphere to that of Venus, Mercury and the Sun with the tip of the Bull's north horn behind in the world of the fixed stars. Furthermore, a week later the Sun, now moving into the Twins, will be opposite Saturn and Uranus who are just about to meet above the tip of the Archer's arrow. Saturn and Uranus are dancing together through the year and this is the second of three meetings, on February 13th, June 26th and October 18th, close to the December solstice point on the Sun's path. Early on the 21st the Sun crosses his June solstice point. Saturn will be clearly visible in the night sky, culminating around midnight when the Sun is on the other side of the earth.

Another visible event will be the opposition of Mars to the Sun on the eve of Michaelmas Day, September 28th. The Sun has just passed his equinox point in the Virgin and Mars is between the two Fishes. When opposite the Sun Mars comes closest to the earth and can be seen as a bright, reddish star also culminating around midnight. Minutes before midnight on September 25th the Moon passes above Mars seven hours after becoming full.

It is worth noting that Venus, Mercury and Mars were in the great line up (also known as the Harmonic Convergence; see chapter 1) around August 24th, 1987, but then all these planets were moving in that greater universe beyond the Sun and this year they come in close to greet the earth. Could this be a challenge for us to work at more clarity towards the extra-terrestial world and its relationship to us and our earth with all her Kingdoms of Nature?

THE DANCE OF THE STARS FROM THE VIEWPOINT OF THE EARTH. 3

In the last chapter we built up a background of the cloak of the fixed star world as it can be observed from the two hemispheres of the Earth, that ever changing wonder of the night sky revolving around those two seemingly fixed points of Polaris above the north pole and a starless area above the south pole. Within the many groups of stars we singled out twelve, those forming the circle of the Zodiac, as being a highway in front of which we can observe the planets or wandering stars with their manifold rhythms. The leader of the planets is the Sun, who shares the quality of the fixed stars through having his own light but appears to us to set the pace of the dance of his fellow planets around the Earth; they receive his light and shine it out adding their individual qualities. We spoke of the gratitude we owe the Sun for giving us the basis of our life in unfailingly marking out our day of 24 hours and year of 365 days. We noted how his living breathing rhythms could only be squeezed into our dead time-pieces by taking Mean Time and inserting leap years. Thus we have two visible movements of our Sun, the second of which can only be seen indirectly. First the east-west arc of the Sun as part of his daily movement, and at the same time a slower west-east change against the background of the stars of the Zodiac which carries him through the twelve constellations in the time-span of a year. Now, within the year there is the change of the seasons. What brings this about? Why does the daily curve of the Sun vary in the course of the year as seen from the same place on Earth?

To try and answer this question let us take two balls to represent Sun and Earth and mark on them a north and a south pole and an equator (Fig. 12). Observation of Sun spots has revealed that the Sun rotates once around his axis in about 27 days. His equator lies on the same plane as his yearly path of apparent movement round the Earth known as the ecliptic. Now stand the two balls up so that the poles are parallel, then move the Sun round the Earth. If this were so the Sun would shine most

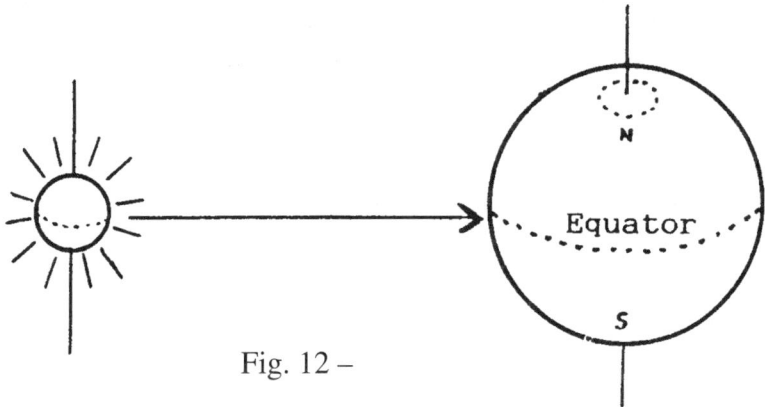

Fig. 12 –

directly on the equator of the Earth for the whole year and there could be no changing seasons, the Sun's rays always falling at the same angle on any particular area of the Earth. But because the Earth is an individuality she inclines the axis of her poles to that of the Sun by 23½°; thus the plane of her equator is also inclined to that of the Sun, the ecliptic (Fig. 13). If you now do this with your two balls and again move the Sun around the Earth you will find a time in the year when the rays of the Sun fall more directly on the northern hemisphere (June) and another when they are more directed to the southern part of our Earth (December). This brings about summer

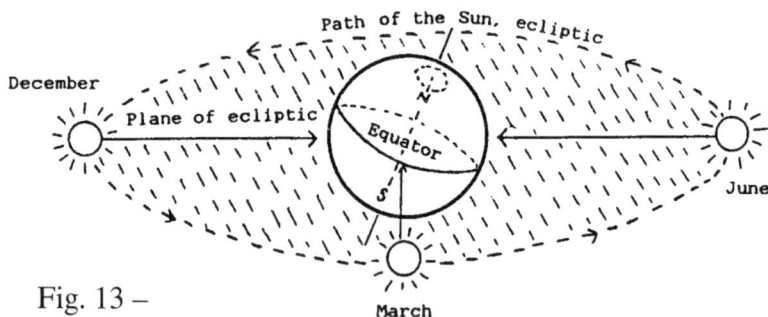

Fig. 13 –

with its mid-point at the solstice giving the longest day (in the north) as the Sun rises north of east and sets north of west, traversing a long arc culminating high above the horizon. In the winter the opposite conditions take place and these two alternate in the two halves of the Earth, with the variations between day and night increasing as one moves away from the equator. Exactly between the two solstice points on its yearly circle the Sun's rays fall directly on the meeting point of the planes of the two equators. This is the moment of the equinoxes (March and September) when day and night are of equal length over almost all of the globe and the Sun rises due east and sets due west. The Sun then circles the Earth above the equator whereas in June he circles the Earth north of the equator above what is marked on a globe as the Tropic of Cancer and at the opposite solstice point in December he has moved south to circle above the Tropic of Capricorn (northern hemisphere, reverse for southern regions). We shall see later why these two names are used.

This circle of the Sun's yearly course around the Earth has been given its starting point at the vernal equinox as it marks the commencement of spring in the Northern hemisphere. In earlier times, especially among the Celtic peoples, the movement of the Sun through this point where the two planes of the Sun and Earth meet called forth a special celebration to inaugurate the beginning of a new year. Two or three centuries before Christ the ecliptic was divided into twelve equal divisions of 30° each which were given the same names (or symbols representing those names) as the fixed

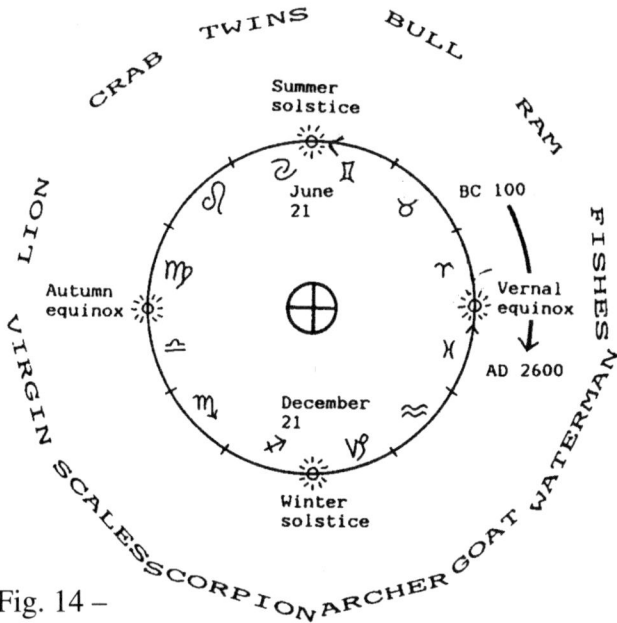

TWINS BULL

CRAB

Summer
solstice

RAM

LION

June
21

BC 100

VIRGIN

Autumn
equinox

Vernal
equinox

FISHES

December
21

AD 2600

SCALES

Winter
solstice

WATERMAN

SCORPION ARCHER GOAT

Fig. 14 –

star groups of the Zodiac. In these articles the divisions of the ecliptic will be referred to as signs to distinguish them from the unequal† star constellations of the Zodiac. Thus the Sun enters the sign of Ram or Aries at the vernal equinox, the sign of Crab or Cancer at the summer solstice, the sign of Scales or Libra at the autumn equinox and the sign of Goat or Capricorn at the winter solstice (Fig. 14, where appropriate symbols are given. All seasons as in the northern hemisphere). This is why the path of the Sun over the Earth at the two solstice times are designated as the Tropics of Cancer and Capricorn on globes and maps of the world.

This will raise a further question, for it will be seen from Fig. 14 that when the Sun enters the sign of Aries at the end of March the group of stars in the Zodiac behind him is that of the Fishes. We now come to a third rhythm of the Sun which marks out much longer periods of time, that of the 'Ages' each comprising about 2160 years. If one could observe the Sun against a particular fixed star when he rose at the time of the vernal equinox one would find a slight change taking place, much smaller than the daily one which marks out the year This movement appears as a very slow moving back, a clockwise change in the relationship of the vernal point to the Zodiac. Each degree of change takes 72 years; thus for the vernal point to move through the whole Zodiac, 25,920 years must pass and this is known as a Platonic year. Readers of Rudolf Steiner will surely have come across his references to the 72 years in connection with the average lifetime of a human being and the secrets of the breath and

---

† There is a difference of oppinion about the size of the visible constellations.

blood circulation hidden in the number 25,920. This precession of the vernal point, and indeed all points along the Sun's yearly path or ecliptic, is brought about by a kind of wobbling movement of the axis of the poles of our Earth. If we could extend the north pole out to the fixed star world and put a giant pencil on the end of it that could write on the heavens it would draw a circle from the north star, Polaris, round the constellation of the Dragon, which holds the extended pole of the Sun, returning

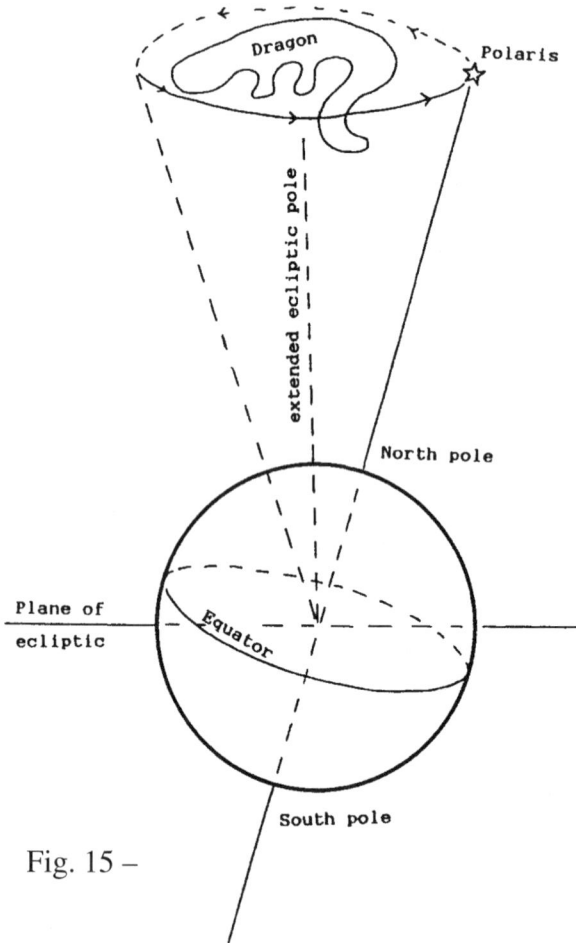

Fig. 15 –

in 25,920 years to Polaris. A similar circle would be traced out by the south pole (Fig. 15).

This 'wobble' also causes the two equinox points to move in the opposite direction against the stars of the Zodiac, bringing about the precession of the equinoxes. Rudolf Steiner has called such meeting points 'gateways' giving access between two spheres. Here we would have gateways from our Earth sphere to that of the greater Sun represented by the visible Sun. Thus it can be seen that these are open to different directions in the Zodiac at different times, allowing special impulses to flow in through the Ages. About 100 B.C. the vernal gate moved from the Ram into the Fishes where it still is and will be until about 2600 A.D. when it will move into the Waterman. If you imagine the whole inner circle of the ecliptic in Fig. 14 moving as indicated by the arrow but then go back in time so that the beginning of the sign of the Ram is where it says 100 B.C. you will see that around the time of Christ the signs were almost coincident with the fixed star constellations bearing the same names. Thus at the first Easter, on Easter Sunday morning (about 10 days after the equinox) the Sun would have risen in front of the stars of the Ram and within the Ram sector of the ecliptic when that mighty Impulse was born into our Earth. Since that time that direct gateway has been modified and will continue to be for a long span of time. Could we entertain the thought that when signs and constellations again coincide we could have so worked with the Christ Impulse that we as mankind could shine something new into the realm of the greater Sun?

Maria Thun with her years of research work observing plant growth and the movement of the Moon through the signs and constellations has come to the conclusion that the plant world is connected with the constellations and not with the signs. Maybe the signs have more to do with challenges offered to mankind. Obviously it cannot be the Sun entering the sign of the Ram which directly awakens the plant life in spring, for that does not happen in the southern hemisphere. However at both equinox times we often experience storms in the atmosphere of the Earth and our world of feelings is closely connected with that realm. Perhaps when we have gained a little more control over our emotions we shall be able to help bring a little more

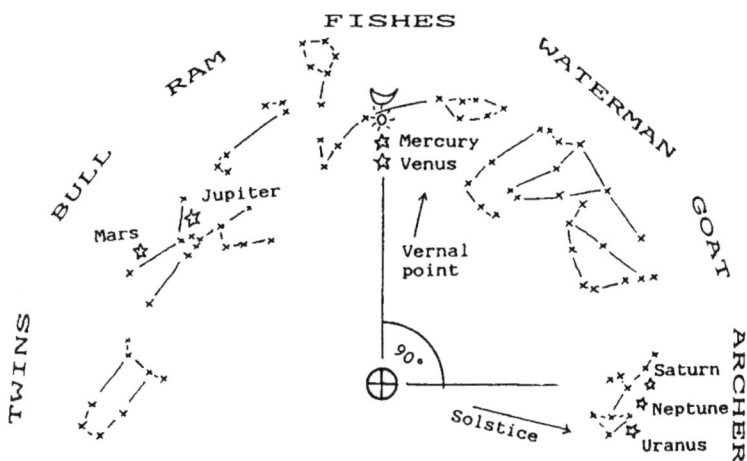

Fig. 16 –   April 6, 1989

harmony into the chaos of that realm at the moment.

Looking at current events in the starry world we can again find two in 1989 taking place near the equinox and solstice positions of the Sun. Saturn performs a dance with Neptune similar to the one he has been doing this year with Uranus, bringing about three meetings through their looping gestures: on March 3, St John's Day (June 24) and November 13. These will all be in the constellation of the Archer and in the first half of the ecliptic division of the Goat or Capricorn. About a month later, April 4, the Sun will meet with Mercury and Venus to be joined by the New Moon two days later. This event will be at a 90° angle to Saturn and in the sign of the Ram or Aries. Mercury and Venus will be below and beyond the Sun (Fig. 16) between the two Fishes. Easter Sunday is almost as early as it can be this coming year, as the Full Moon takes place two days after the Sun enters the sign of the Ram, so that the following Sunday is then on March 26. The first Saturn-Neptune meeting would sound out the preparation and the April 4-6 event will fall in that time when we remember the teaching of the Risen Christ to His disciples.

THE DANCE OF THE STARS FROM THE VIEWPOINT OF THE EARTH. 4

In this chapter we will turn our attention to our nearest celestial companion, the Moon. Everyone is aware of the changing size of the Moon, and a certain number of us notice that it appears at different times of the day and night, but perhaps not so many could form a clear picture of how this comes about. Let us first take the phases of the Moon and follow the cycle from one full Moon to the next. Here again balls or roundish fruit can be an aid to getting the imagination alive. Place a ball in the middle to represent our earth. Then put the ball representing the Sun at a distance from the earth and, at first, let it remain still as we move another ball round, closer to the earth, to represent the movement of the Moon. (If done in a dark room a torch can very effectively represent the Sun.) Starting at full Moon the Moon ball would be on the other side of the earth, opposite the Sun with the disc of the Moon appearing fully lit from our earth view. Moving the Moon anticlockwise until it is at 90 degrees to the Sun, one quarter of the circle round the earth, the left half of the disc appears lit up. This is a last quarter Moon, waning or growing smaller. One more quarter of the circle brings the Moon between Sun and earth. Here the back of the Moon is lit up from our point of view, giving new Moon. We often refer to the new Moon when we see it as a tiny sickle in the western sky after Sunset but then it is already two or three days old.

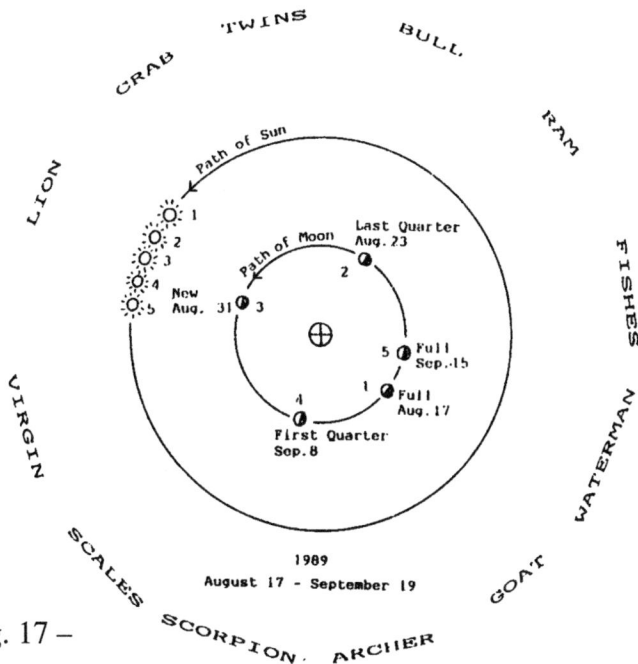

Fig. 17 –

Moving the Moon through a further quarter of its orbit brings it again to a 90 degree angle to the Sun. It has grown to the appearance of a half lit up disc for us, but now the right side is the bright one and we say it is a first quarter Moon, waxing. Another quarter circle brings it back to where we started but now we must add to this the fact that the Sun is also moving and the following full Moon takes place about 20 degrees further on.

Thus the Moon has here two rhythms, a sidereal one of just over 27 days from its position in front of one particular fixed star, round the whole zodiac and back to that same star, and a synodic one of just over 29 days arising out of the Moon's relationship to the Sun, from phase to phase, for example full Moon to full Moon as just described. The movement of Sun and Moon in relationship to the background of the zodiac from the full Moon on August 17th 1989 to the following full Moon on September 15th is represented in Fig. 17. Numbers 1-5 denote simultaneous positions of Sun and Moon.

If you have used a torch to follow the Moon phases you will have become aware that the earth gets in the way of the Sun's rays and throws a shadow on the Moon at full Moon, and that at new Moon the disc of the Moon covers the face of the Sun as viewed from the earth. Thus you will have discovered eclipses. However this does not happen every full and new Moon. Why not? Again we must add another fact to our picture. The orbit of the Moon is inclined by five degrees to that of the Sun. Therefore it cuts through the plane of the path of the Sun, or ecliptic, in two diametrically opposite places called the Moon nodes. Where the Moon rises above the ecliptic plane is designated the ascending node (☊) and where it moves below, the descending node (☋). Thus the Moon rises to being five degrees higher or descends to five degrees below the Sun's path between the two nodes, and twice a month will be on the same plane while passing through the nodes. The Sun in its yearly course will pass behind one of the nodes about every six months. When at these times the Moon is also there it will give, at full Moon, a total Moon eclipse due to the shadow of the earth, or at new Moon a total Sun eclipse with the Moon passing between earth and Sun. Partial eclipses can take place if the Sun is within a certain distance of the nodes. On August 17th the Sun will be within one degree of the descending Moon node and therefore the shadow of our earth (which is always present!) will cover the Moon between 2.20 a.m. and 3.56 a.m. GMT, bringing about a total eclipse visible wherever the Moon is above the horizon. For about one hour before and after the total eclipse the shadow will gradually cover and uncover the face of the Moon.

With a Sun eclipse the cone of the shadow of the Moon just reaches the earth, making a narrow path up to 160 miles wide over varying parts of the earth and it can only be observed within a certain distance of that path. At the time of new Moon on August 31st, the Sun will have moved about 11½ degrees beyond the descending Moon node, near enough to bring about a partial Sun eclipse with the greatest coverage of the Sun's disc at 5.45 a.m. GMT. This will only be visible from extreme S.E. Africa, Madagascar and part of Antarctica. (A total Sun eclipse lasts only a few minutes; a total Moon eclipse can last up to four hours).

The Moon moves in an elliptical path and is therefore at times nearer to the earth, in perigee, or further away, in apogee. The apparent size of the discs of Sun and Moon is almost exactly the same, about half a degree, so that when a total Sun eclipse occurs with the Moon near perigee the whole face of the Sun is covered. However when the Moon is near apogee there is still a rim of light visible from the disc of the Sun as the Moon then appears slightly smaller. This is called an annular eclipse.

Yet another rhythm must be added to these phenomena. The orbit of the Moon moves round on the plane of the ecliptic so that the nodes change their relationship to the constellations of the zodiac moving clockwise (the opposite way to the Sun and Moon) by about 1½ degrees in a month. A complete revolution of each node through the zodiac takes 18 years and seven months. Thus the two periods when the Sun passes behind the nodes is about three weeks earlier each year. A smaller rhythm belongs to the perigee and apogee, which are also known as the apsides. These points on the Moon's orbit move anti-clockwise through the zodiac by an average of about three degrees for each orbit of the Moon, amounting to over 40 degrees each year and taking about nine years for a complete revolution. These are not constant forward movements but complicated oscillations with a prevailing forward movement. This is so with the nodes but even more complicated with the apsides as there they do

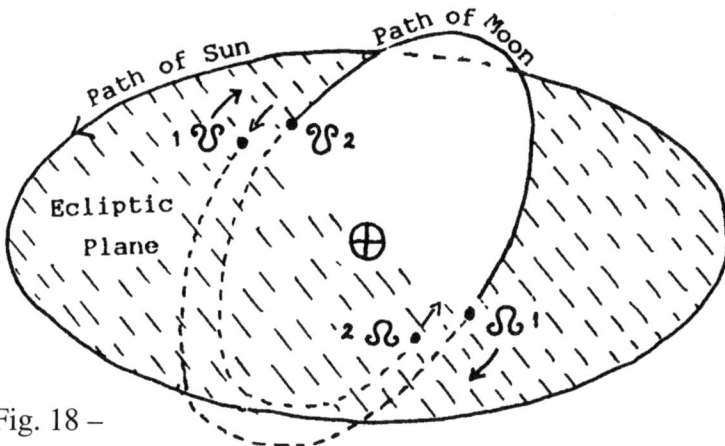

Fig. 18 –

not take place simultaneously, but alternately, so that the perigee and apogee are not always directly opposite one another in the zodiac. Nothing stands still in the cosmos and the manifold rhythms manifest its inherent life! (See Figs. 18 and 19).

The Moon sphere, that is, the 'sphere' enclosed by the Moon's orbit, is the last stepping stone from the spheres of the cosmos to the earth, and the Moon nodes can be seen as gateways from the great universe with the Sun and planets to the realm of our earth. From this one can have some understanding of the importance of these particular rhythms both in the life of man and of the earth. In the planting calendar by Maria Thun we are advised not to sow when the Moon is passing through one of its nodes, as the extra-terrestrial forces streaming through these gateways are not helpful to plants at those moments. I once inadvertently sowed a lawn on the day of an eclipse and was afterwards horrified to witness the struggle the little seedlings had to grow into straight healthy blades of grass.

Another indication given in some planting calendars is the Moon's highest and lowest position. This is when the Moon is passing through those constellations of the zodiac where the Sun follows its highest and lowest arc in the sky within the cycle of the year. In the northern hemisphere the Sun is highest at mid-summer when entering the Twins and lowest at mid-winter when entering the Archer, these being the two

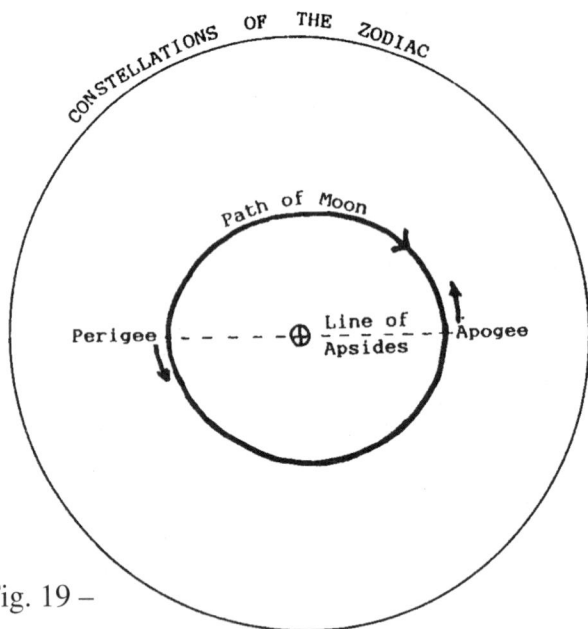

Fig. 19 –

solstice points (for southern regions it would be the reverse, see pages 23, 24). Within the yearly cycle of the Sun the Moon passes through these constellations every month and appears to manifest something of the same quality as the Sun then displays, their respective rays falling at the same angle on our earth.

These are some of the main rhythms of the Moon. However there are very many finer fluctuations which make calculations of the Moon's orbit very difficult. The Moon has an intimate relationship with all the planets, particularly through the Sun, as each conjunction or opposition of the Sun with a planet affects the Moon's movement, accelerating or retarding it.

From November 13th to 16th, 1989, there are remarkable starry events taking place between the constellations of the Archer and the Twins. On November 13th, Saturn and Neptune meet for the third time this year The following day Jupiter moves opposite them in the Twins; this is the second of three oppositions of Jupiter to Saturn which take place only every 60 years in this part of the zodiac. The other two are on September 10th, 1989, and July 13th, 1990. Two days after the opposition, on November 16th, Saturn and Neptune will be joined by Venus, and Jupiter by the waning Moon, which was full on November 13th. Venus with Saturn above her is then visible low in the south-western sky after Sunset until they too set about three hours later (if the horizon is flat). To the eye of imagination Neptune would appear just above

Fig. 20 –

Saturn and Uranus a little to the right, all in front of the Archer. Opposite, north of east, the Moon will rise about 3½ degrees above Jupiter in front of the stars of the Twins, remaining visible most of the night. (For southern regions the relative positions of the planets must be reversed). (See Fig. 20.)

Saturn, Uranus and Neptune were last together in the Archer 500 years ago, from 1487 to 1490 at the time of the Renaissance. The pictured image of this portion of the starry sky which has come down to us from an earlier period of civilization is that of a centaur. The upper part of man rising out of the lower animal nature and aiming with bow and arrow at the preceding constellation of the zodiac represented by a scorpion, the creature that holds the secrets of death within its tail but also the secrets of the overcoming of death, those of resurrection. Jupiter has been moving through the same part of the fixed star world as during the three years when the Christ walked our earth in the body of Jesus and has reached where it was shortly before the Deed of Golgotha. Saturn is moving into the position opposite where it was at the Baptism. Such thoughts can perhaps help us to meet these silent challenges in a constructive and truly human way.

THE DANCE OF THE STARS FROM THE VIEWPOINT OF THE EARTH. 5

In the last chapter we wrote about some of the rhythms of the Moon. Readers may read what John Soper wrote in the Letter[†(see end of Chapter)] section about the ascending and descending rhythms of the Moon as experienced in the middle part of the earth between the tropics of Cancer and Capricorn. I am grateful to him for pointing out that the earth must be looked at as a threefold being, having an upper, middle and lower region as has man. I can understand the significance of having a celestial body, especially the Sun or Moon, directly overhead as I was fortunate enough to experience this with the Sun while going by ship to New Zealand. It was an unforgettable experience standing one day on deck and suddenly becoming aware that I had no shadow; added to that, I was surrounded by a golden sea of reflected sunlight. Perhaps there are some other readers living and working with the earth in this middle region who can offer experiences or start now to observe such cosmic events.

We will now turn our attention to the two inner planets, Venus and Mercury. They are both very attached to the Sun, Venus never moving more than 48 east or west of him and Mercury staying still nearer, within 28 . This means they only appear in the night sky as morning or evening star, rhythmically alternating between these two. Unlike all the other planets they can never even be at right angles to the Sun, let alone opposite, and so can never be above the horizon at midnight. Their gestures are similar as they circle the Sun as he moves around us but their different qualities manifest in the geometrical figures which they draw out. Let us first follow the movement of Venus. To trace out the full pattern she weaves around us on earth as we view her meetings with the Sun we must follow her for eight years. Going back to January 1986 we find her in superior conjunction with the Sun, beyond the Sun with both planets just moving into the constellation of the Goat (Fig. 21, I). Venus, moving faster than the Sun, gradually pulls ahead during the following nine months until there are about 30 between them. Then it seems as if she feels she is getting too far from her celestial companion and so sweeps in nearer to the earth going back to meet the Sun in inferior conjunction in November 1986 (Fig. 21, II). Now she is moving between Sun and earth in front of the constellation of the Scales. Completing her looping gesture Venus now chases after the Sun, moving out beyond his path until she catches him up again in superior conjunction. This meeting was very near the bright star Regulus in the constellation of the Lion on August 23, 1987 (Fig. 21, III).

And so the dance continues with an inferior conjunction in the Bull, June 1988 (Fig. 21, IV), followed by a meeting beyond the Sun in front of the Fishes, April 1989 (Fig. 21, V). Thus during the course of the last four years Venus met the Sun in five different directions within the circle of the Zodiac, three superior and two inferior conjunctions. The next meeting will take place in January 1990, again between the constella-

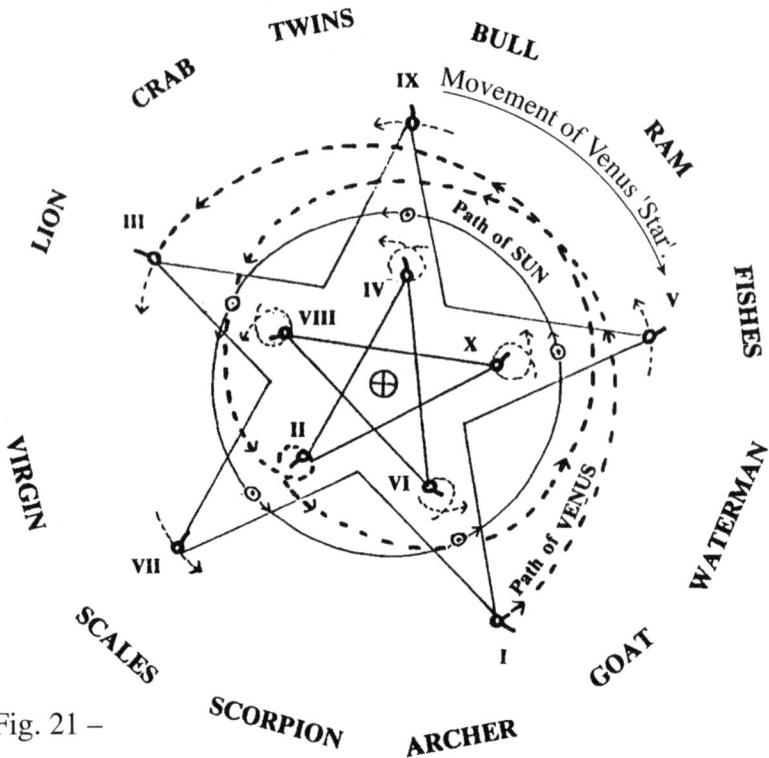

Fig. 21 –

Constellation labels around the figure: TWINS, BULL, CRAB, RAM, LION, FISHES, VIRGIN, WATERMAN, SCALES, GOAT, SCORPION, ARCHER. Movement of Venus 'Star', Path of SUN, Path of VENUS. Points labelled I–X.

tions of Archer and Goat, similar to that in 1987 but this time it will be an inferior conjunction with Venus between Sun and earth (Fig. 21, VI). The dance goes on with an outer meeting before the Scales in November 1990, a loop in the Lion, August 1991, a superior conjunction in the Bull, June 1992, and an inner meeting in the Fishes, April 1993 (Fig. 21, VII-X). With this the pattern is completed giving five outer meetings and five inner meetings in front of the Goat/Archer, Scales, Lion, Bull and Fishes. The following meeting in January 1994 will be an outer one in front of the Goat/Archer in a near similar position to the one we started with in 1986. If we take those ten meetings and join the five inner and five outer points we can form two stars with five rays each, or we could also picture a five-petalled flower. Then we must not forget that we on our earth are in the middle and are rhythmically being clothed with this wonderful, harmonious pattern.

To this beautiful geometric form we must add the life of the cosmos and then we find that those five rays do not always shine towards the same constellations of the Zodiac. That great 'star' turns slowly within the Zodiac circle so that in the course of about 1,200 years each corner reaches out towards all twelve constellations. It moves counter to the Sun's yearly movement as in the course of time the meetings take place slightly earlier, 2¹/₃ days every 8 years, with the Sun 2°3' further back. Thus the superior conjunction in January 1994 will have just moved back into the constellation of the Archer from that of the Goat. This pentagram is a very harmonious figure with almost exactly 72 between each ray and takes about 240 years (8 x 30) to move a fifth of the circle. All these gestures and forms can become much more alive if one draws or paints them but especially by moving them with music or singing.

Venus is by far the brightest of all the planets and fixed stars. She can even be seen during the day in certain favourable positions. Visibility as evening star occurs about 36 to 40 days after a superior conjunction when Venus is pulling away eastwards of the Sun and therefore setting later. That will depend on which constellation she is in and how that is viewed from any particular place on Earth. When the retrograde movement takes place, which can be found in any ephemeris, this can be followed against the fixed star background until Venus vanishes into the light of the approaching Sun. It can then be seen that the planet traces out variously shaped 'loops', including hairpin curves, according to which part of the Zodiac they take place in. About three weeks after the inferior conjunction Venus will reappear in the morning sky having moved to the west of the Sun and so rising first. She remains as morning star until about 5 weeks before the superior conjunction, vanishing again into the light of the Sun as she catches him up. In earlier times a distinction of quality was expressed between Venus appearing in the evening sky as Hesperus and as morning star Phosphorus.

Venus has phases, similar to the Moon, some of which can be observed with a small telescope or binoculars. New Venus occurs at inferior conjunction with the Sun and full Venus at the superior meeting. The fact that this planet appears quite a bit larger at new Venus than at her full phase means that she reaches her greatest brilliance when appearing in a crescent form as evening star between her greatest elongation (further distance from the Sun) east and the new phase. She then changes to morning star and again reaches greatest brilliance between the inferior conjunction and reaching greatest elongation westward of the Sun (Fig. 22a & 22b). This apparent change of size occurs because Venus is six times nearer to the Earth in her loop than when in superior conjunction. It is worth noting that the crescent forms appear in reverse order to those of the waning and waxing Moon. The positions of Venus within the circle of the Zodiac at greatest elongation east or west and at greatest brilliance as evening or morning star also appear in their own pentagonal form, emphasizing this quality of the Venus sphere.

In the next article we will contemplate the planet Mercury. Let us now take a brief look at the cosmic situation during the twelve Holy Nights between December 24, 1989 and January 6, 1990. As can be seen in Fig. 3, all the planets, except Jupiter are moving in the regions of Scales, Scorpion, Archer and Goat. Jupiter, opposite the Sun on December 27 and therefore at his brightest, will be the only planet above the

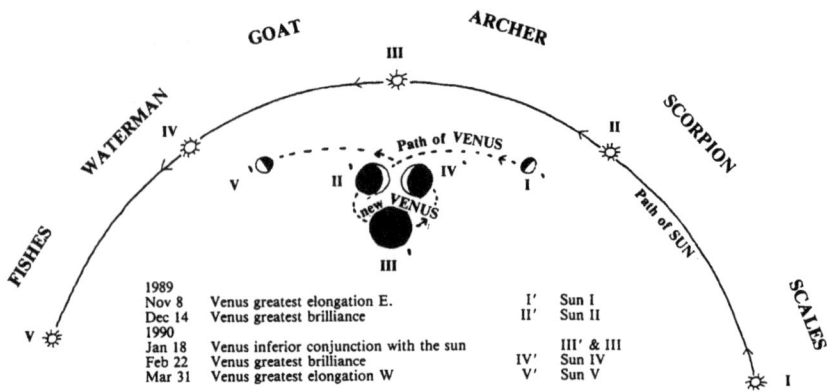

GOAT
ARCHER
III
WATERMAN
IV
SCORPION
Path of VENUS
V
II
IV
I
new VENUS
Path of SUN
FISHES
III
SCALES
V

1989			
Nov 8	Venus greatest elongation E.	I'	Sun I
Dec 14	Venus greatest brilliance	II'	Sun II
1990			
Jan 18	Venus inferior conjunction with the sun	III' & III	
Feb 22	Venus greatest brilliance	IV'	Sun IV
Mar 31	Venus greatest elongation W	V'	Sun V

I

EARTH

Fig. 22 a –
Paths of Venus and the Sun from Nov 8, 1989-Mar 31, 1990

horizon at midnight December 24/25. He will shine out from the feet of the Twins, the Sun's midsummer position in the northern hemisphere, and look across, beyond the earth, to those five planets gathered in the Archer. Because of their looping movements Jupiter and Saturn come directly opposite each other twice during this year, September 10 and November 14, and a third time next year on July 13, 1990. These 'great oppositions' take place only every 60 years in the same constellation of the Zodiac. There were three similar oppositions

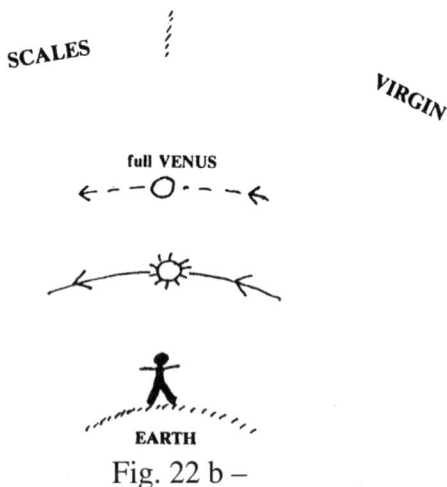

SCALES

VIRGIN

full VENUS

EARTH

Fig. 22 b –

during 1930-31 which was the time when Hitler and Mussolini were rising to power.

Last year the Moon was full on December 23 and thus waning through the twelve Holy Nights until new Moon on January 7, 1989. This year new Moon falls on December 28 and she will be waxing towards full Moon on January 11, 1990. Between Christmas Eve and the last day of the year she will move from the constellation of the Scales to that of the Goat, meeting with all eight planets there and passing opposite to Jupiter. These are obviously especially challenging times but as was pointed out in the last star article we can gain ample help by contemplating Jupiter sounding out from

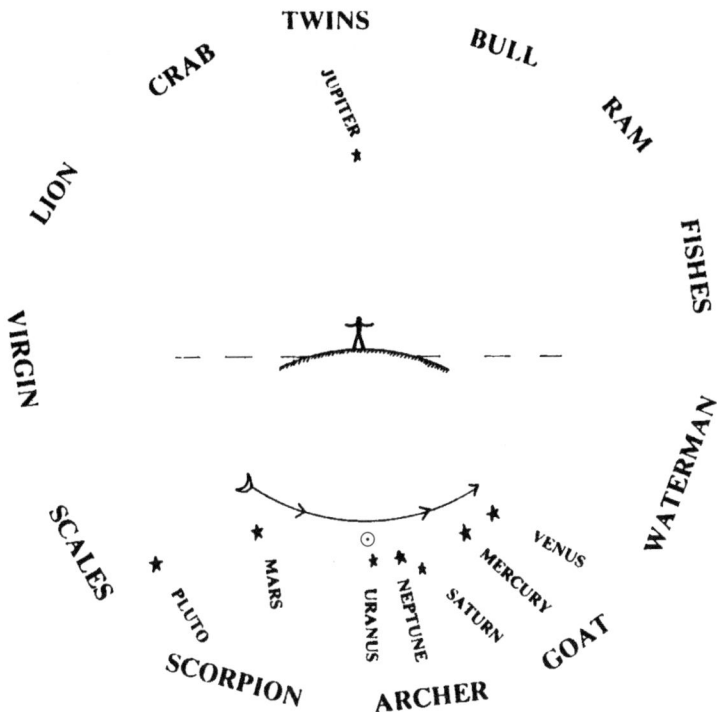

Midnight December 24/25, 1989

Path of moon from December 25-30, 1989

Fig. 23 –

a similar position to where he was around the time of the first Easter and Saturn moving opposite where he was at the Baptism of Christ by John the Baptist.

† LETTER

Moon in the Tropics

Dear Editor,

As soon as one enters the tropics celestial conditions are quite different from those in the temperate regions, though it seems that this obvious fact cannot for some peculiar reason be grasped by people who have spent most of their lives in Central Europe, Britain or N. America. They talk glibly about northern and southern hemispheres divided by the equator. But there are in fact three earthly zones -northern from the N. pole to the tropic of Cancer, southern from the S. pole up to the tropic of Capricorn, and the large tropical zone between the two tropics. At every point in the latter during the course of a year the mid-day Sun will be directly overhead twice except at its turning points in June and December: the dates when this occurs will vary according to latitude. As the monthly path of the Moon, give or take a degree or two, coincides with the annual course of the Sun through the zodiac, it follows that it too will be directly overhead twice a month: sometimes it will move thence northwards, sometimes southwards, but always descending. So a BD. grower in the tropical zone wishing to work with the ascending and descending rhythm will have to puzzle out for himself how it might apply to his particular degree of latitude, and not expect others to tell him.

It is a moot point whether this Moon rhythm is of any practical significance in the tropical zone. Certainly there is no hint of this in the local traditions of the natives of East Africa or Malaya. However some do, or used to, work with the waxing and waning periods, ...

John Soper 24th March 1989

THE DANCE OF THE STARS FROM THE VIEWPOINT OF THE EARTH. 6

In the last chapter we looked at some of the characteristics of one of the two inner planets, Venus. Now we will consider her close companion Mercury. Although they share many similarities they have their own very distinct qualities. The Greek name for Venus was Aphrodite, the goddess of love who was born out of the foam of the sea as portrayed in Botticelli's famous painting 'Birth of Venus'. Mercury was known as Hermes, the messenger of the gods for which task they gave him winged sandals and a winged cap that he could deliver their messages with all speed. These brief descriptions of Venus and Mercury come to expression in the quality of their movements. Harmony shines out of the pentagram star arising from the dance of Venus. Mercury has many more hidden aspects but he is much faster than Venus and does not find it important to weave such regular forms. Both are very attached to the Sun and therefore dance around him as he appears to circle the Earth each year, moving alternatively in between Sun and Earth then out again beyond the Sun towards the fixed stars as we described in the last article. However, the faster speed of Mercury brings about a very different geometrical figure from his meetings with the Sun. Whereas Venus takes eight years to form her double pentagram around us Mercury takes just

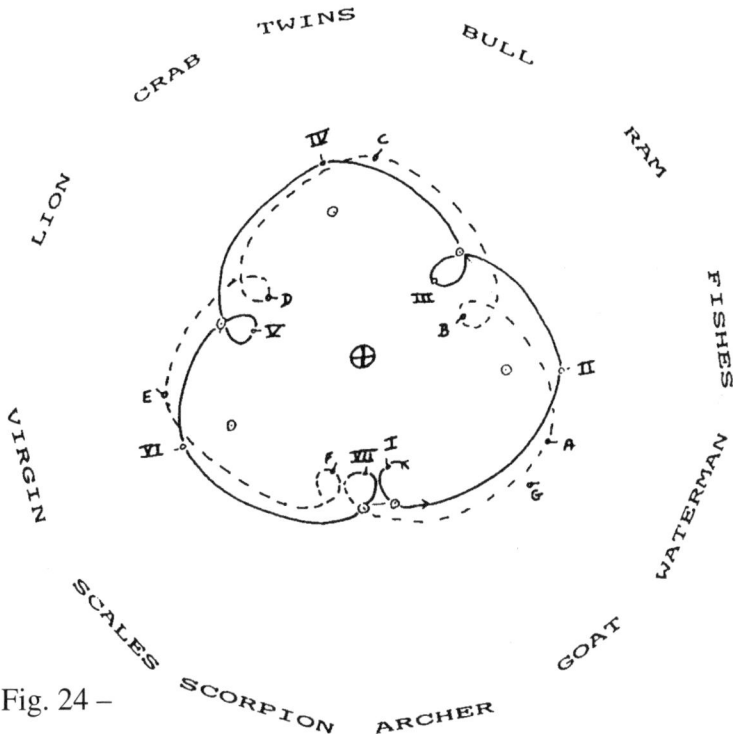

Fig. 24 –

43

under one year.

Let us follow the movements of Mercury and the Sun during 1990 and 1991 to get a feeling for their dance together. On January 1, 1990, both were moving in front of the Archer. Mercury, beginning to feel uncomfortably far ahead of the Sun had come in to greet the Earth and had just started to go back for a reassuring meeting with the Sun. This took place on January 9 (Fig. 24 : I). Finishing the looping movement he then chased after the Sun who had gone on ahead. Sweeping out beyond the Sun's path he caught him up on March 19 before the constellation of the Fishes (Fig. 24:II). And so their game goes on with an inner meeting in the Ram on May 3 (III), an outer meeting before the Twins on July 2 (IV), inner meeting in the Lion on September 8 (V), outer meeting near Spica in the Virgin (VI) and an inner meeting again in the Archer on December 24, Christmas Eve (VII). The dotted line in Fig. 24 represents the path of Mercury during 1991 with meeting A on March 2, B on April 14, C on June 17, D on August 21, E on October 3 and F on December 8. ((G) on February 12, 1992.)

Thus it can be seen that the conjunctions 'drop back' each year by quite a number of degrees. Any one conjunction moves back through the twelve constellations of the Zodiac taking about twenty years to return to the same place. If we now join the positions of the three inner and three outer yearly conjunctions we get two triangles, one nearer to us on Earth enveloped by a more cosmically orientated one, giving basically

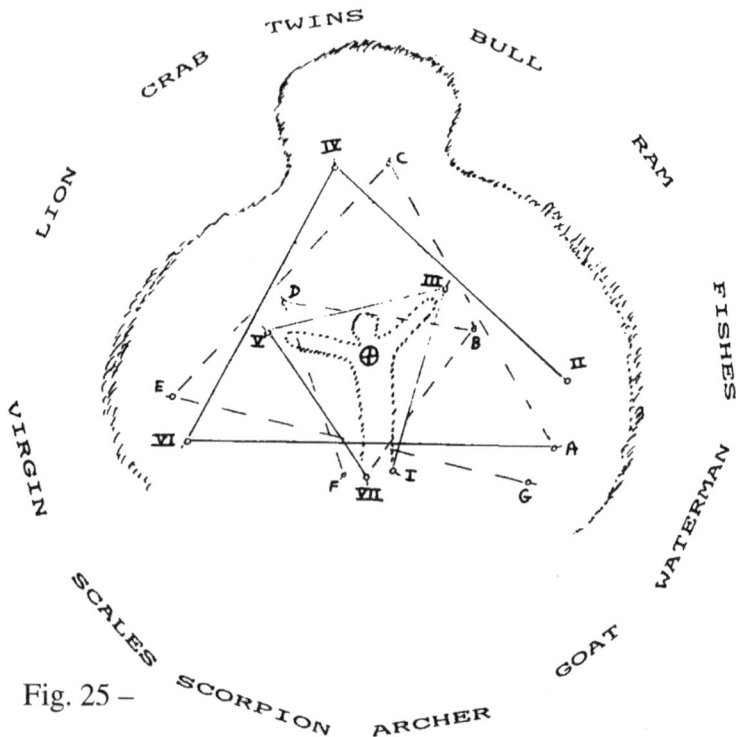

Fig. 25 –

44

the form of a six pointed star or flower. This it is which rotates in a similar way to the pentagram of Venus, only much faster. It can at once be seen that these are open triangles because of the moving on of the conjunctions (Fig. 25). One can also see that the pattern changes year by year. It is not always so beautifully symetrical as this year, 1990. Because the first meeting with the Sun takes place so early in this year, January 9, there are seven conjunctions whereas most years there are only six. There is a seven year rhythm hidden in this changing pattern so if one goes back to 1983 one finds the path of Mercury very similar to this year, with seven Sun meetings, the first, an inferior conjunction, on January 16. A much longer rhythm of 46 years brings a return of the Mercury phenomena with a delay of only one day. Thus in 1944 there was an inferior conjunction of Mercury with the Sun on January 8. This rhythm was already known in ancient times to Hipparchus (c. 190-120 B.C.).

These five and six rayed stars woven by Venus and Mercury can be seen in nature. There are many flowers with five petals but the rose is especially related to the five pointed star, most easily visible in the sepals and petals of the wild dog rose. It is always a magic moment to discover the star within the apple when cut open around its equator. This form is very conspicuous in starfish and etched on the hard covering of the sea-urchins.

The six pointed star appears particularly in the flowers of the lily family, the snow-drop and iris manifesting it with their three small petals encompassed by three larger ones. The bees build their cells on the form of a hexagon which is also revealed in snowflakes when looked at through a microscope. Microscopic pictures of certain species of plankton reveal various forms in the structure of their skeletons, including the hexagram and pentagram. These forms arising from the rhythmic movements of the planets have also been found in the growth patterns of plants, for instance the arrangement of the leaves around the stem, or the scales around the centre of the pine and fir cone. (See article by Joachim Schultz 'On the Phyllotaxis of Leaves', translated by Katherine Castelliz Published in the booklet *Spiritual Influences in the Kingdoms of Nature and in Agriculture* by Elidyr Press in 1981.).

As Venus is the brightest of the classical planets and most easy to observe so Mercury is the most elusive. Although almost as bright as Sirius, the Dog-star, his constant nearness to the Sun means that he is never visible in the sky outside the region of bright twilight setting in his evening star period soon after the Sun and as morning star rising shortly before sunrise. His elongations west or east of the Sun are between 18 to 28 whereas the greatest possible elongation of Venus is 48°. With the aid of a telescope Mercury can be seen to go through phases similar to those of Venus (See Fig 22a & 22b in 'Dance of the Stars', last chapter .).

The size and shape of the loops vary in the different regions of the Zodiac. The retrograde movement is shortest in the constellation of the Bull, 8½°, and longest in the opposite constellation of the Scorpion, up to 16½°. The shape varies from a more open or closed S form to a real loop. If the paths of the planets lay on the same plane as that of the Sun (the ecliptic) with each inferior conjunction the planets Venus and Mercury would pass across the Sun's disc. That this does not always happen is due to the fact that the orbits of the planets are inclined to that of the Sun and therefore only coincide in two places, the ascending and descending nodes similar to those of the Moon. Venus is only inclined by a modest 3½° but Mercury by 7°, the strongest inclination of all the planets with the exception of Pluto at 17°. This means that such a transit as it is called can only take place when the planets and the Sun are in or near a node. Then, with the aid of a small telescope (not looked at directly!) Mercury or Venus can be seen to move across the disc of the Sun as a small black spot. The ascending and descending nodes of Venus seen from the Earth are now in the regions of the Scorpion and the Bull and transits can only happen when the two planets are within 1½° of one of these points. This does not happen very often but in a rhythm of 8, 121½, 8, and 105½ years. The last one took place in 1882, December 6, and the next will be on June 7, 2004, in the Scorpion and the Bull.

The ascending node of Mercury lies in the Scales from the viewpoint of the Earth and his descending one in the Ram; transits of the Sun by Mercury can occur when both planets are within 3½°. A central transit can take up to 5½ hours whereas with the slower moving Venus it can last up to 7 hours. Mercury transits occur more often, in intervals of 7, 9½, 3½, 9½, 3½ and 13 years with an occasional interruption in the cyclic sequence. The last was in November 1986 and the next will be in November 1993, both in the Scales.

The most outstanding starry event of this year seems to be the third of the threefold clarion call of the oppositions of Jupiter and Saturn. We have mentioned this twice before, also the striking events immediately before where Saturn had threefold meetings with the outer planets Uranus and Neptune. However, the more one contemplates these great signs in connection with the momentous world events now taking place the clearer they sound out. The great opposition takes place on July 13, the next day the Sun moves opposite Saturn and is conjunct with Jupiter on July 15. Jupiter and the Sun in the Twins are supported on either side by Venus in the Bull and Mercury in the Crab. Across, on the other side of the Zodiac, Saturn is still accompanied by Neptune and Uranus, all in the Archer (Fig. 26). Perhaps the word opposition can have a misleading implication of conflict but one could also think of the possibility of something new arising out of a reconciliation. Duality was a necessary part of evolution and is expressed in the image of the Twins, with their two bright stars Castor and Pollux, the mortal and the immortal Twin. Jupiter and the Sun will be moving below Pollux (above in the southern hemisphere). The seed for the healing of the great division was laid by the deeds of the Christ during the three years he worked on the Earth manifesting through the body of Jesus. These events were proclaimed by Saturn moving through the Twins at the time of the Baptism and Jupiter in his

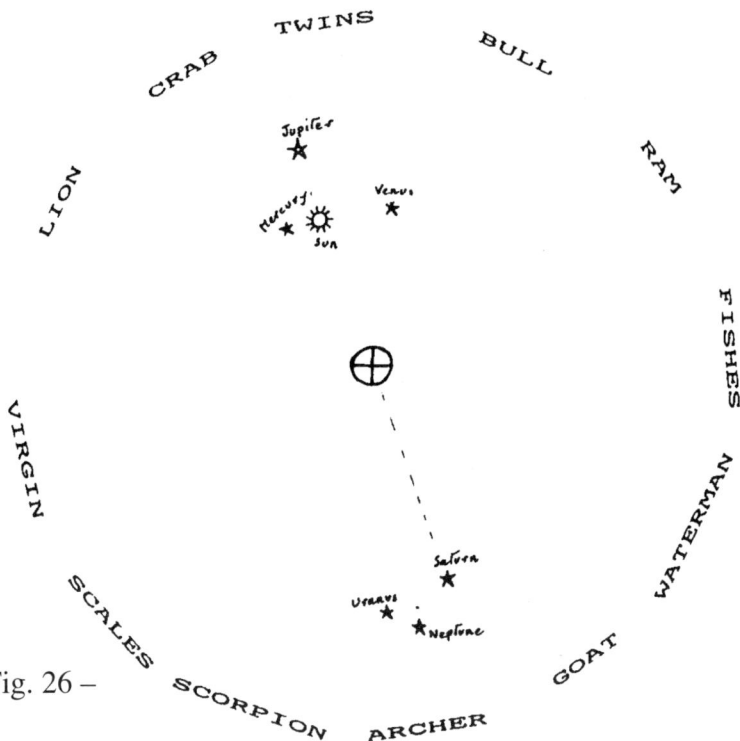

Fig. 26 –

CRAB TWINS BULL
LION RAM
VIRGIN FISHES
SCALES WATERMAN
SCORPION ARCHER GOAT

Jupiter
Mercury Venus
Sun
Saturn
Uranus
Neptune

present position at the culminating deed of union with the Earth on Golgotha in 33 A.D.

The cosmic rhythms of the relationship of Jupiter and Saturn behind this present event take us back to a great conjunction in 7 B.C. The Three Kings, out of the royal star wisdom they still bore from the time of Zarathustra very likely read this as the most important of many signs announcing the beginning of a new era with the rebirth of their great leader as the Jesus child they later went to worship. Going back only 60 years to the previous threefold opposition of Jupiter and Saturn in the Twins - Archer will remind pupils of Rudolf Steiner how he spoke of the promised second coming of Christ about to take place in the mid thirties. Not again an appearance through a physical body but 'in the realm of the clouds' as it is described in the Acts of the Apostles, the realm of life which for a long time has been hidden behind the sense perceptible world.

The great circle of the Milky Way representing the plane of the greater galaxy within which we swim in our Solar System cuts through the Zodiac circle in the Twins and the Archer. Could this be looked on as the 'gateways' of majestic 'nodes' challenging us to raise our view of world events to cosmic dimensions, to the realm of life?

THE DANCE OF THE STARS FROM THE VIEWPOINT OF THE EARTH 7

In past chapters we have looked at the movements of the whole starry heavens as we observe them from the earth. Also the individual movements of Sun, Moon and the two planets intimately connected with the Sun, Venus and Mercury. Moon, Venus and Mercury all move faster than the Sun on whose circuit through the twelve areas of the constellations of the Zodiac we base our year. We now turn our attention to the so-called outer planets and we will first consider the rhythms and gestures of Mars. Mars shares some of the characteristics of both the outer and inner planets. Like Venus and Mercury he moves sometimes in the space beyond the Sun and at other times comes closer to us than the path of the Sun. However, moving slower than the Sun he does not mind at times being opposite to him in the circle of the Zodiac. These events happen when Mars comes closer to the Earth in a looping gesture. This takes place about every two years and then Mars is at his brightest, a full Mars, similar to the full Moon as we see his fully lit up side from the earth. Then Mars rises at Sunset, setting at Sunrise, and is visible throughout the night. This brightness varies in intensity according to where in the Zodiac circle the opposition takes place. Mars is closest to the earth and therefore at his greatest brilliancy when the opposition takes place at the end of August with Mars in the Waterman and the Sun in the Lion. Some readers will perhaps remember 1988 when the opposition of Mars with the Sun took place early on Michaelmas Eve, September 28. Although the loop was formed in front of the stars of the Fishes, Mars was clearly visible in his retrograde movement, brightening from his usual smaller reddish appearance to an orange-yellow glow brighter than Jupiter, before dimming again over the following weeks. As these oppositions occur only every 15 years in similar positions within the Zodiac he will not appear so bright again during this century. In between the oppositions the Sun catches up with Mars in conjunction, Mars being beyond the Sun. He remains invisible for at least six months around the time of a conjunction, outshone by the Sun and mostly above the horizon during daylight hours. These are biyearly events as also with the oppositions.

Mars is in greatest contrast to the harmonious movements and gestures of Venus, indeed he shows irregularities and variations both in space and time to a degree not found in any other planet. Therefore the time between conjunctions and oppositions can vary by almost 50 days; likewise his distance from the earth is also variable, with his greatest distance being sometimes about seven times that of his nearest.

Fig. 27 shows the path of Mars over four years, from 1988 to 1992. To gain a deeper experience of these rhythms try tracing the movements of Sun and Mars simultaneously with a finger from each hand. With the Sun finger start on the Sun's path in front of the Archer, where the Sun is moving at New Year, and for each of the four years

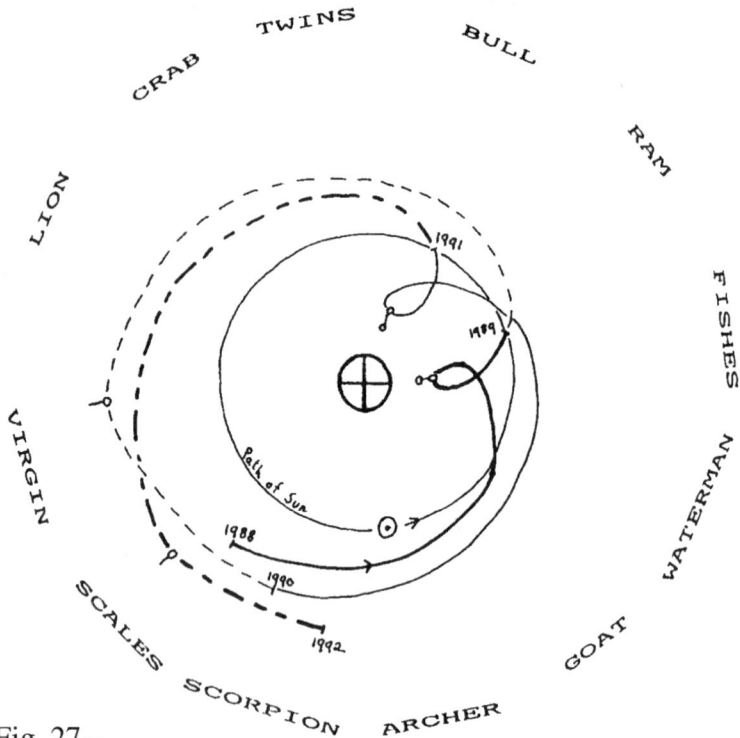

TWINS

CRAB

BULL

LION

RAM

1991

1989

FISHES

VIRGIN

Path of Sun

1988

WATERMAN

1990

SCALES

1992

GOAT

SCORPION   ARCHER

Fig. 27 –

Annual path of the Sun and the path of Mars from 1988 to 1992

make the circuit of the Zodiac. While the Sun finger follows this movement the Mars finger, starting at the beginning of 1988 in the Scales outside the Sun's path, sweeps in to be near the earth when the Sun reaches the Virgin for the moment of opposition. Then Mars proceeds to the 1989 point on his path while the Sun completes the circle back to the Archer. Continuing on through 1989 the Sun catches up Mars in the Virgin, Mars has now swung out beyond the Sun for the conjunction which took place on Michaelmas Day. The Sun moves on again to the Archer and Mars to the Scorpion for the beginning of 1990. The opposition in 1990 takes place on November 22 with Mars looping in the Bull and the Sun in the Scorpion. By the end of the year Mars is just coming out of his loop but still in the Bull and the Sun has again returned to the Archer. In 1991 the Sun catches up Mars for a conjunction on November 8, this time in the area of the Scales. By New Year 1992 with the Sun again in the Archer, Mars has proceeded to the end of the Scorpion area of the Zodiac. Don't forget that we are observing this dance from our earth in the middle of this map! An even more alive presentation is for two people to walk the planet paths with a third observing them from the centre point of the Earth. Why not also try doing the same for the Sun and

Mercury as pictured in the last chapter.

In Fig. 28 the positions of the conjunctions and oppositions of the Sun and Mars are given from 1985 to 2001. They are numbered in the order of the events taking place and show how in a rhythm of 15 years the conjunction or oppositions returns to a similar direction in the Zodiac. In each case this takes place in seven steps, the eighth sounding the octave. As can be seen by comparing 1 and 15, 2 and 16, the events are not exactly repeated every 15 years. Only after 79 years do they recur about 3½ days later in a very similar but not identical position in the Zodiac. Most of times given are only to the nearest year whereas the exact rhythms always contain fractions of a year. More exact figures can be found, for example, in *Movements and Rhythms of the Stars* by Joachim Schultz or *Astronomy and Imagination* by Norman Davidson.

The loop formations vary between an S or Z gesture when occurring where the path of Mars rises above or sinks below the plane of the ecliptic and a real loop where his path is furthest above or below that of the Sun. The crossing points of the two planes of movement change very slowly against the background of the Zodiac and at present Mars rises above the ecliptic in the region of the Ram and descends again in front of

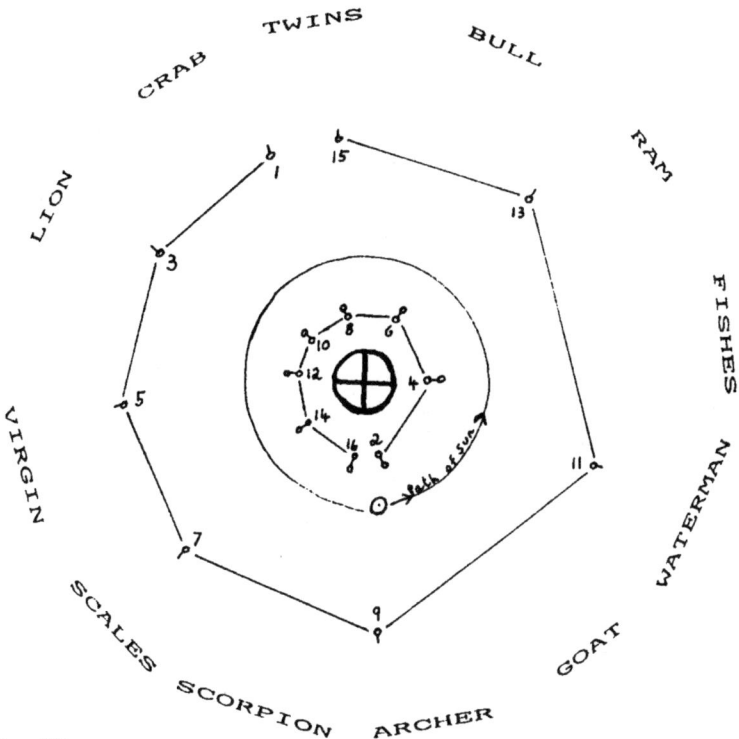

Fig. 28 –

Conjunctions and oppositions of Mars with the Sun
from 1985 to 2001

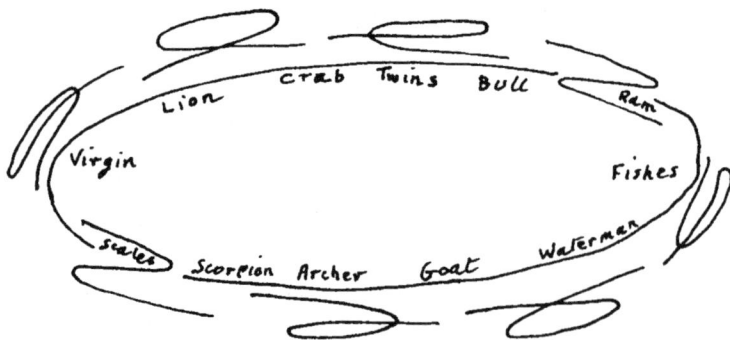

Fig. 29 –

Representative loop forms of Mars

the stars of the Scales. This is schematically pictured in Fig. 29 where the zigzag form becomes an increasingly open and upward loop gesture culminating in the Crab-Lion area where the path of Mars reaches its highest point above the ecliptic, gradually returning again to an S or Z in the Scales. The same sequence of form is repeated from the Scorpion to the Fishes with the loops being formed downwards. (For the southern hemisphere reverse above and below, up and down and turn Fig. 29 upside-down.)

The gesture of Mars around the time of his opposition to the Sun on November 27 of this year is pictured in Fig. 30 against the background of the stars of the Bull. Since very ancient times the quality connected with this direction of the Zodiac has been closely linked to the two star clusters of the Pleiades and Hyades and the brighter, reddish star Aldebaron marking the eye of the Bull. Aldebaron is sometimes rendered the Follower, that is of the Pleiades, and also God's Eye. Almost exactly opposite is that bright, even redder, star Antares, the heart of the Scorpion, that constellation which is said to be the birthplace of the planet Mars. Antares means 'rival of Mars' or 'similar to Mars' and the alchemists said that iron could only be transformed into gold when the Sun was in the area of the Scorpion. At the time of the opposition the Sun will be passing near Antares. The ancient Persians looked to Aldebaron and Antares as two of the Four Royal Stars, their Four Guardians of Heaven, the other two being Regulus and Fomalhaut.

As can be seen in the diagram Mars is leading us into the coming year with a zigzag gesture between the star clusters of the Pleiades and Hyades with Aldebaron. Clouds permitting we will see him pass Aldebaron three times, about September 25, November 13 and February 21, moving slightly further away each time. He is nearest to the earth on November 20 and therefore at his brightest. Mars marks New Year's Day by coming out of his retrograde movement and proceeding again forwards. Seventy-nine years ago, in 1911, there was an opposition of Mars to the Sun on November 25. Mars was very near the Pleiades, about 3 degrees further back than this year's opposition, and the Sun had just entered the Scorpion. For students of Rudolf Steiner it is enlightening to note that during the time of that loop of Mars in 1911 he spoke of the deeper aspects of evolution in a very special way. Rudolf Steiner challenged us to understand the role of what we term 'evil' so that we can play our part in transforming it into positive fruits for the future. Behind the Scorpion's sting of death lie the secrets of Resurrection; behind the powerful forward charging Bull lie the secrets of the Creative Word. What wonderful imaginations Mars offers us to carry into 1991.

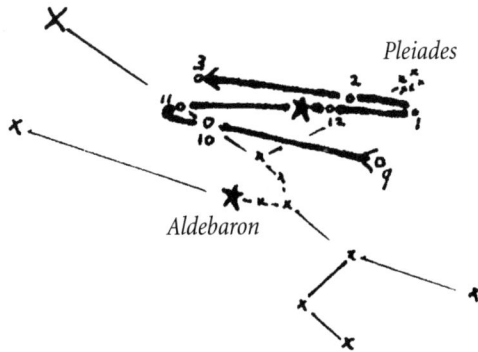

Fig. 30 – *The path of Mars from September 1990 to March 1991 Point of opposition, November 27, indicated by ★ on the path of Mars.*

THE DANCE OF THE STARS FROM THE VIEWPOINT OF THE EARTH 8

Last time we considered Mars and noted that although he belongs to the so-called outer planets he shares some of the characteristics of the inner planets Mercury and Venus. Now we shall turn to the two outer planets Jupiter and Saturn, looking at some of their similarities and at each as an individual. Like Mars they both move more slowly than the Sun and do not mind being on the other side of the Zodiac to him, which the inner planets cannot bear owing to their very close connection with the Sun. However when Mars is opposite the Sun, which happens every two years, he sweeps in close to the Earth, nearer than the path of the Sun. Owing to their still slower speed, Jupiter takes almost 12 years to move round the Zodiac and Saturn almost 30; they move opposite the Sun once every year. At that time they nod in towards the Earth in a looping gesture but never come as near us as the Sun, nor is it as near as Mars at his greatest distance from the Earth. Every year the Sun overtakes them, Jupiter and Saturn being far behind the Sun from our point of view but invisible, as with all the planets when in conjunction, in the light of the Sun. They are at their brightest, full Jupiter and full Saturn, when opposite the Sun and visible all night; rising as the Sun sets and setting at sunrise. Between conjunction and opposition they will be at right angles (quadrature) to the Sun. They reach this relationship shortly before moving back in looping gesture and three to four weeks after the loop has been completed.

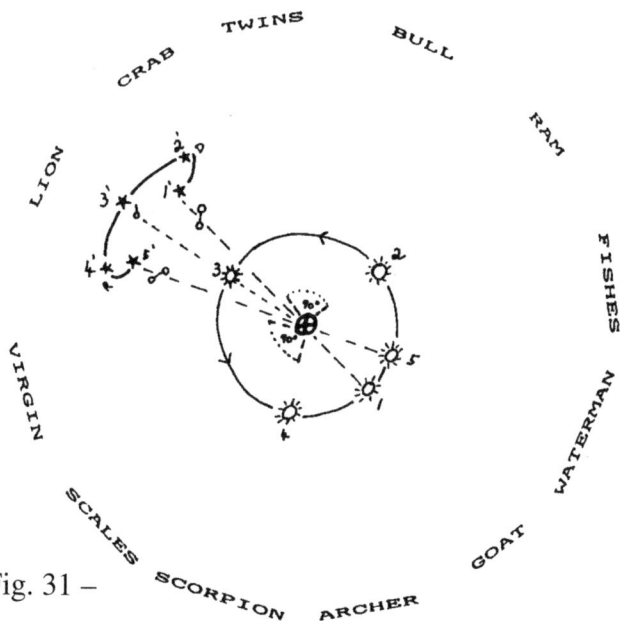

Fig. 31 –

55

In Fig. 31 the paths of Jupiter and the Sun are shown between their opposition on January 29, 1991, and the following one in 1992 on February 28. Try taking two markers and following their paths simultaneously or, better still walk them with two friends one of whom sits on the Earth. If there are twelve others they can represent the constellations of the Zodiac! Starting in position 1 for the Sun and 1' for Jupiter, the Sun will proceed from the Goat to the Ram but Jupiter will first move retrograde (R), in the opposite direction in the Crab until just before 2' when he turns and moves in the same direction as the Sun which is termed direct (D) in the Ephemeris. When they, or perhaps I should say you, reach 2 and 2' Jupiter and the Sun will be in quadrature with a 90 angle between them. Now both continue in the same direction until the Sun catches up Jupiter in the Lion, 3 and 3', when they are conjunct (σ). Now the Sun pulls ahead reaching quadrature again when he is in the Scorpion with Jupiter still in the Lion: 4 and 4'. The Sun continues moving in the same direction to position 5 while Jupiter is slowing down, becoming stationary, and then moving again in the opposite direction to the Sun (R). When the Sun reaches position 5 in the Waterman, Jupiter is directly opposite (σ^{o}) in the Lion; 5'. Thus it is that the oppositions, and also the conjunctions, progress through the Zodiac returning almost, but never exactly, to the same position after 12 years. In 1979 there was an opposition of the Sun and Jupiter in the Waterman-Lion on January 24, five days earlier than this year's on January 29 and therefore about 5° further back. In 2003 they will be opposite each other on February 2, near the transition from the Crab to the Lion with the Sun five degrees further into the Goat.

Let us add now how we will be able to see Jupiter in the sky this year, or any other synodic period as his relationship to the Sun is called. This is usually taken from conjunction to conjunction which takes about one year and one month. As we noted above Jupiter is at his brightest in opposition to the Sun, full Jupiter, and obviously rises at sunset, setting at sunrise. This year that happened on January 29. Then, as the Sun moves towards Jupiter and Jupiter moves at first towards the Sun, Jupiter will rise always a little earlier than sunset until they both reach position 2,2 on Fig. 31' on April 25, then Jupiter will culminate as the Sun sets and we will see him to the south as the sky grows dark. When the Sun is directly below at midnight Jupiter sets in the west. Between the positions 2 and 3 the Sun comes nearer and nearer to Jupiter who sets always earlier and finally is only visible in the west just before sunset soon to vanish into the rays of the Sun as they reach conjunction, August 17, and set and rise together. Now the reverse happens as the Sun gradually pulls ahead of Jupiter and Jupiter begins to rise before the Sun in the eastern sky becoming visible as morning star. When they again reach quadrature (4,4') on December 6, Jupiter will rise at midnight and be in mid-heaven when the Sun rises. Soon after this Jupiter turns retrograde and the two move further apart before becoming opposite again (5,5') on February 28, 1992. Before this he will rise earlier and earlier before midnight until, in opposition, he rises as the Sun sets. It can help to picture this from the diagram if you take a piece of paper and move it firstly as a horizon for the rising and setting Sun in the five given positions. Thus you can follow the gesture of Jupiter against the background of the Crab and Lion except for the month of August when he is too near the Sun to be visible.

Fig 32 shows the paths of Saturn and the Sun between two conjunctions: January 18, 1991(1,1') and January 29, 1992 (5,5'). Readers can follow the gesture of Saturn in a similar way to that described for Jupiter. Numbers 2,2' indicate quadrature (90°) on April 27; 3,3' opposition on July 27; and 4,4' quadrature on October 24. It can easily be seen how the slower movement of Saturn gives a much smaller yearly movement and loop than the gesture of Jupiter over about the same period. The synodic rhythm of Saturn, from one conjunction with the Sun to the next is about one year and two weeks. Thus these conjunctions, and the oppositions which take place in between, move around the Zodiac returning to about the same place every 29 years. In 1962, on January 22, Saturn and the Sun met four degrees further on in the Goat and in 2020 they will meet on January 13 about five degrees further back than this year, at the end of the constellation of the Archer.

These particular gestures of Saturn and Jupiter have been chosen because there is a very special event taking place this year between these two planets. Because of their different rhythms of revolution through the circle of the Zodiac, every 20 years they meet or become opposite. This takes place in front of three different constellations of the Zodiac. In the last chapter, we spoke about the third of three oppositions which took place during 1989/90. Owing to the looping gestures of these planets such events often take place in a threefold way. Going back 20 years we find another great opposition which took place three times during 1969/70 (see Fig 33). Saturn ($\hbar$) was then in the Ram and Jupiter ($\jupiter$) in the transition between Virgin and Scales; Twenty years earlier, 1951/2,

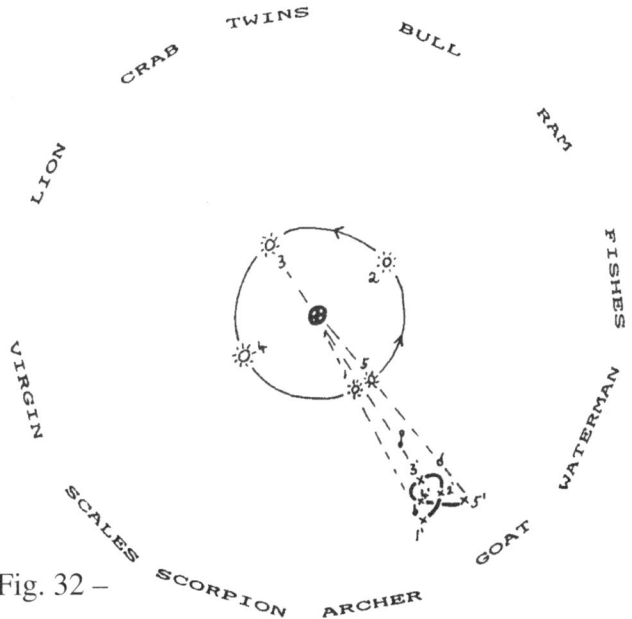

Fig. 32 –

57

Saturn had a threefold conversation from the Virgin with Jupiter in the Fishes. Going back a further 20 years, 60 from now, we find Saturn in the Archer in a similar position to 1989/90, looking across three times to Jupiter in the Twins.

Joining the points where Saturn moved during these events a three cornered star arises as a mathematical but invisible reality. As these oppositions do not take place in exactly the same relationship to the stars of the Zodiac but fall back a little each time, this 'star' rotates. This is a very slow anticlockwise movement like threefold hands on a great cosmic clock, each hand or corner taking about 2500 years to move through the whole Zodiac and return to a similar position.

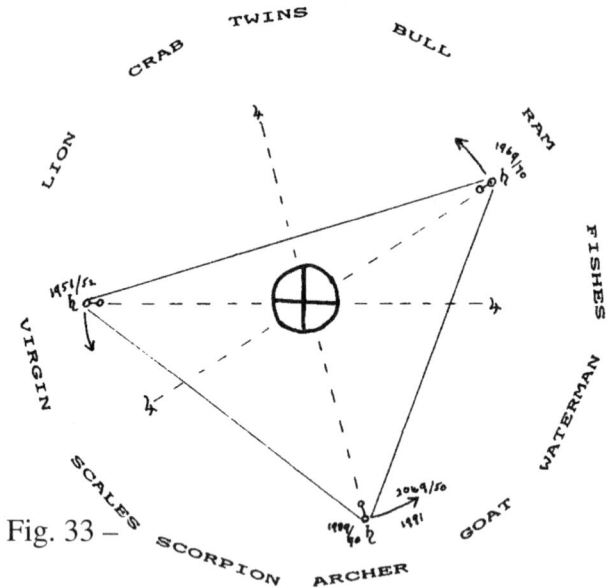

Fig. 33 –

The very remarkable thing about this present series of oppositions is that this year there will be two more of these great conversations on March and May 16. It is almost as if there was a pause to allow the first sounding out to fully resound and then again a further twofold reminder making it a fivefold event. Obviously Saturn and Jupiter have moved on since the last of the first three calls on July 13 of last year. This time Saturn has entered the region of the Goat and Jupiter that of the Crab, almost exactly where they will be in 60 years time when the next threefold opposition will take place in 2049. During 1989/90 Saturn was looking across to Jupiter in the place from where he proclaimed the great event of the Baptism in Jordan, the beginning of the Three Years. This year Saturn will remind us of the culmination of those Three Years when he looks across to Jupiter moving near to where he was during the original Easter Events.

As we work at deepening an understanding of our Earth and her needs we can perhaps do well to ponder on that great Deed which the Spirit of the whole Universe fulfilled on our planet Earth.

THE DANCE OF THE STARS FROM THE VIEWPOINT OF THE EARTH 9.

We now come to consider the three outermost planets of the family of the Solar System, Uranus, Neptune and Pluto. They share the same characteristic gestures of Jupiter and Saturn but move at a very much slower pace. Let us first consider Uranus whose orbit is further from us than that of Saturn. Since ancient times Saturn has been considered to be the outermost planet in our Solar System. However, in 1781, William Herschel was living as a musician in Bath, England, and also working at his abiding passion of astronomy. He was also able to build more refined telescopes than were in general use at that time and on March 13 of that year he trained one of these on the constellation of Gemini. There he noticed one of the faint stars which did not appear as a point of light but as a tiny disc. Watching it from night to night he observed that it moved in relationship to the other stars of Gemini or the Twins. First he thought he had found a comet but on calculating its path it was found to be orbiting beyond that of Saturn. Herschel called it 'Georgium Sidus' in gratitude to King George III who gave him a grant to carry on his research. However, Bode, well known for his law concerning the distances between the planets, suggested Uranus as being the mythological father of Saturn and this name was later adopted. Possibly the symbol ⛢ is connected with the first letter of Herschel's name.

Uranus takes about 84 years to loop his way round in front of the twelve constellation of the Zodiac, nodding in towards the Earth each year when he moves opposite the Sun. Thus he takes about 7 years to traverse each constellation. It has since been discovered that the axis of the planet Uranus lies almost on the same plane as his orbit whose obliquity to the plane of the Earth differs by only 0.8 . Thus he would present to the Earth first one pole, then a nearly vertical equator with a pole to each side, then the other pole in the course of 86 years. About 1986, when Uranus was moving in front of the Scorpion, his north pole was pointing towards us on Earth. It is now thought that he rotates on his axis about every 17 hours but in the reverse direction to the Earth. 15 Moons have been detected at least some of which orbit every few days above the equator of Uranus.

Galileo was the first to 'see' the planet Neptune in his telescope at the end of 1612 however he did not realise that it was a planet. He was observing Jupiter and its satellites and added what he thought was a fixed star noting at the bottom of his sketch that one star had 'seemed further apart' from another the night before. Much later this was thought to have been Neptune who had just started to retrograde near Jupiter in the Virgin. Galileo was not able to follow up these observations to realise that this moving star was a planet and Neptune was to orbit nearly 1½ times before being identified by Johann Galle at Berlin Observatory on the night of September 23, 1846. Neptune circles the Zodiac every 164.8 years and was then moving in the region of the Waterman. Johanne Galle had taken calculation of the French astronomer Le Verrier for another planet had been assumed to exist because of gravitational disturbances of the orbit of Uranus. Thus Neptune was finally discovered on the basis of calculations. Under ideal conditions Uranus is just visible to the naked eye whereas Neptune can only be observed through a telescope and Le Verrier, who had sent his calculations to the Berlin Observatory, named it Neptune, after the god of the sea. Quite unknown to Le Verrier an English astronomer, John Couch Adams, had already completed similar calculations only due to a delay at the Cambridge Observatory where he had sent them his were not confirmed until later.

Uranus and Neptune have often been described as twin planets having a similar bluish colour with Uranus being slightly larger and both considerably larger than our planet Earth. The orbits of both deviate only slightly from the plane of movement of the Earth (or Sun), Uranus 0.8 and Neptune 1.8 , less than any of the other planets. When Voyager 2 flew past Neptune in 1989 it beamed back messages which were interpreted as describing a dynamic and stormy world arising out of the Great Dark Spot thought to be a tremendous storm centre in its southern hemisphere. This was likened to the Great Red Spot on Jupiter, an area described as an intense windstorm three times larger than the Earth. Eight Moons have been observed the biggest of which, Triton, described as colourful and orbiting in a reverse direction as with some of the Moons of Jupiter and Saturn.

Pluto has still a different history of discovery. Deviations in the paths of Uranus and Neptune led astronomers to search for a tenth planet further out. Percival Lowell in America, among others, spent many years at the beginning of this century calculating then observing from his private observatory in the clear air of Arizona. After his death in 1916 members of his staff carried on the search. However it was not until 1930 his faithful follower Clyde Tombaugh, using a special device called a blink microscope†, announced on March 13 that he had tracked down another planet in the constellation of the Twins. This discovery was made by studying photographs and the planet was then called Pluto, ruler of the Underworld. One of the two signs used for this Planet (♇) also form the initials of Percival Lowell. But the ironical thing about this discovery is that shortly after it was found what had been hailed as a supreme success of mathematical astronomy was in fact due to Tombaugh's painstaking search. The calculations were reexamined and the discrepancies in Uranus's orbit were found to be more likely to have been tiny errors in measurements before more refined ways had been found as new measurements of Pluto's mass showed figures too small to have any discernible effect on the other planets. Its elliptical orbit brings it within the near circular path of Neptune for 20 years of its 248.5 year circuit of the Sun. This happened last in January 1979 and it will only regain its position as the outermost planet of our solar system in March 1999. The plane of his movement deviates by 17° from the Sun-Earth plane, 10 more than Mercury who had otherwise by far the biggest deviation of the planet family, whereas Uranus and Neptune have the smallest as noted above. In 1978 James Christy of the US Naval Observatory discovered a large Moon which he named Charon, after the boatman of mythology who ferried souls across the Styx. Charon is over a third of Pluto's size and orbits him every 6.4 days, the same rotation time as Pluto himself therefore he hangs over one spot on Pluto's surface. Pluto and his Moon present Astronomers with many puzzling peculiarities which are not shared by any other members of the solar family. Recently it has been discovered that all the outer planets, except Pluto, have rings. Pluto was at his highest above the ecliptic (below for the southern hemisphere) in 1980 as he passed 17 08' above (below) Spica in the Virgin. He is now moving about 15 above (below) the stars of the Scales and will enter the Scorpion area in July 1994 still about 13 above (below) the ecliptic. Only in the next century will Pluto cross the ecliptic at his node when in the constellation of the Archer, then continue for the next 124 years below (above) the path of the Sun. Uranus and Neptune are close together in the Archer, Uranus just below (above) and Neptune just above (below) the ecliptic. Uranus catches up Neptune on February 2 for the first of three meetings during 1993, due to their looping gestures. Two years later Uranus moves into the Goat followed by Neptune in March 1997.

† Blink Microscope – Which causes any object that has moved, on otherwise identical photographs, to appear to jump. (*Atlas of the Solar System*, David Hardy).

THE GREAT COSMIC SUNFLOWER

From Astronomy we often hear of our little Earth as an insignificant member of the Solar System, a mere speck of dust in space. From popular Astrology humanity can be seen as ruled by the planets, unable to do more than accept their situation, although it is true that the more enlightened astrologers do suggest the possibility of self-transformation to a certain degree. However, there is rarely a view expressed which gives an inspiring thought towards a greater aim of existence. Out of the background of Rudolf Steiner's Spiritual Science and the further working out of this by my friend and teacher Willi Sucher (1902 - 1985), I would like to offer the following picture of the Universe, especially of our Solar System

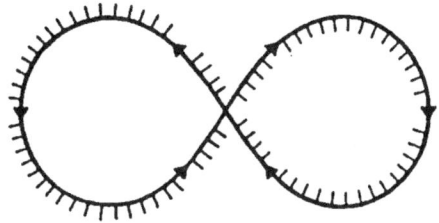

We cannot actually observe the Copernican or Heliocentric view of the Universe, wherein the Sun is considered the still point, with the planets, including our Earth moving around it. However, with our thinking we can reconcile that idea with our actual obser-

Fig. 34 –

vations. Consideration of some of the phenomena connected with the Sun can lead us to think that we may have to change our usual expectations of behaviour. Perhaps it would help first to follow through the remarkable path of a lemniscate Fig.34. If we 'walk' one end of the figure, being aware that our right arm, if extended, would point out to the space around, and then continuing through the crossing point, we find that the same right arm pointing into the inside of the figure. In some mysterious way outer and inner have become reversed. Something like that appears also in connection with the Sun.

When there is a Sun eclipse, with the Moon blotting out the seeming disc of the Sun, there appears around the darkened area a beautiful shining light known as the Corona. This is such a special sight that on those occasions astronomers from many parts of the world take their instruments to the very best viewing spot to catch a glimpse of

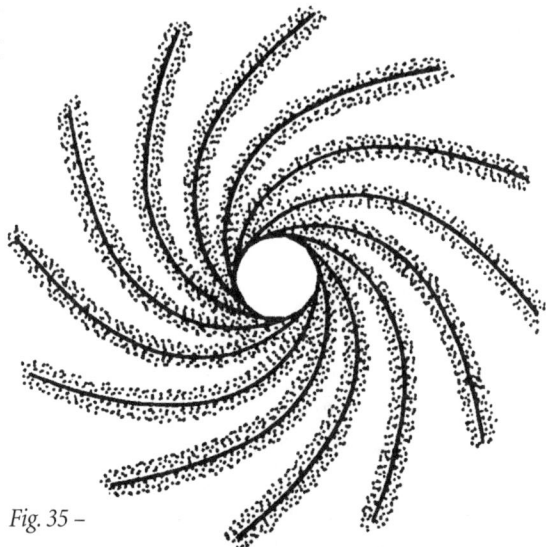

Fig. 35 –

this appearance which mostly lasts only a few minutes. The shape and size of this light area varies, and this appears to be connected with sunspot activity. Some astronomers have suggested that it actually extends over the whole solar system. Another astonishing feature of the corona is that it is found to have temperatures of over a million degrees centigrade, compared with those on the disc of the Sun which are only six thousand degrees. This heat is also described as activity, and the picture arises of the surrounding of the Sun being infinitely more active than the disc itself from which we usually expect this activity to ray out. Earlier in this century an astronomer by the name of Raymond A. Littleton came to the conclusion , through the results of his observations, that the corona represents material falling in towards the solar surface! It appears to be connected with the 'zodiacal light' which can be best observed in the tropics after sunset or before sunrise. This appears as a cone of light, of similar quality to the corona, which shines up in front of the zodiac, and on rare occasions reaches across the whole arc of the zodiac which is above the horizon at that time.

Sunspots have been recorded by Chinese astronomers since earliest times, but a closer look at this phenomenon has only recently been taken. There seems to have been a reluctance to accept the shocking fact that the disc of the Sun could have blemishes! These sunspots have been found to increase and decrease in number with a rhythm of 11 to 22 years, and to be closely linked to happenings on earth, such as northern lights, earthquakes, and disturbances in radio communication. In photos these appear as little vortexes, not always round, which disappear into a dark center as if "Drilled" into the disc of the Sun - another 'reversal,' as the Sun is usually assumed to be emitting light and heat from its center.

Over the last thirty years research has been carried out by bombarding the visible Sun with sound waves. The results of this have led to radical changes in the previous conjecture of the interior of the Sun: the 'core' at least is now considered to be an empty space! Early this century Rudolf Steiner suggested that if one could go to the Sun one would find there not only empty space but a space emptier than that which surrounds it. In a certain respect this is similar to what astronomers term black holes - those terrifying areas which suck everything in from their surroundings, completely annihilating it Fig. 35. However, the astronomers moved on through their research to the concept of white holes, where that which had been annihilated reappears somewhere else. This reminds one of the 'magic' of projective geometry laws, whereby following certain geometric laws one can 'see' a point

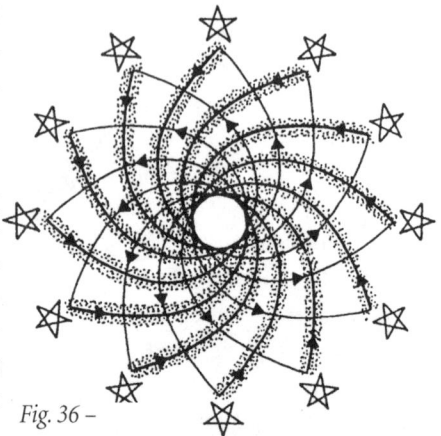

Fig. 36 –

vanish in the centre and reappear at the periphery Fig. 36. To
add just one more thought to
these considerations: could the
disc of the Sun, which appears
so solid at times, particularly
at sunrise and sunset, be similar to the appearance of a soap
bubble? This also has a certain
solidity, but is only a hollow
skin which vanishes completely
when burst.

With these few thoughts by
way of preparation, let us go
back to the time when the solar
family was still united with the
Sun. We can picture the gigantic sucking activity represented

Fig. 37 –

by twelve streams flowing towards the center, or non-center, where they vanish: a
black hole effect. This is the typical gesture appearing in photographs of galaxies Fig.
35. If we now add the reappearing gesture of the hole activity, we could picture it as
in Fig. 36. There we have something with the same dynamics as appear in the plant
kingdom, for instance in the arrangement of the seeds in a sunflower head, or in a
cactus. Thus we come to a picture of two interpenetrating streams representing an
intense twofold activity.

However alive we are able to make this imagination, it is still an endless and aim-
less repetition.
Representing
the inflowing
streams with
twelve people,
we would find

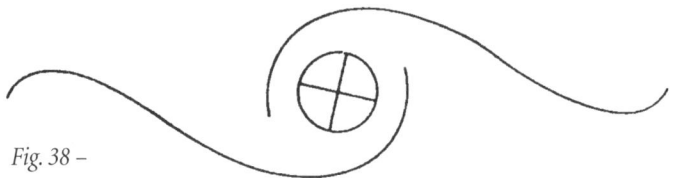

Fig. 38 –

the spaces between them becoming smaller and smaller until the moment when they
stand shoulder to shoulder and can go in no further. With our physical laws of space
there is no way in which the twelve can reach the center together. However, we are able
to complete the process in our thinking, even following the movement through the
vanishing point and returning again to the periphery. Translating this ingoing process
into a wave motion, we would find it cresting at the point of greatest condensation and
then flowing on in a slightly different way as does a wave after it has broken Fig. 38.

Picturing this process in stages, we could think of four steps to the point of intolerable condensation where it 'snaps' or breaks, and two more containing the dissolving element towards the total dissolution in the non-center Fig. 39. Thus we arrive at areas with differing degrees of density, but interpenetrating and coursed through with active streams of movement. Adding the third dimension, we come to a concept of spheres which astronomers describe as being slightly flattened, or lens-shaped. Within the continuing process condensing in each sphere, through the interaction of the two streams, smaller areas

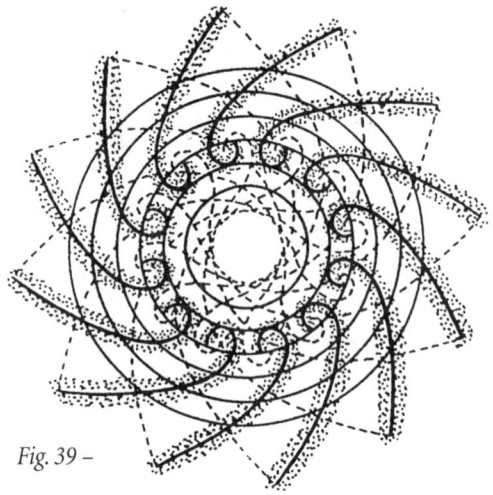

Fig. 39 –

become denser and are set in movement around each sphere. This portrays the birth of the planets within our solar system Fig. 40. These are given weight or density by astronomers, rising in scale from Saturn to the Earth, and then decreasing again through Venus and Mercury. Thus we have come to a picture of the Heliocentric, or Sun-centered view of our solar family, as presented by Copernicus. For Copernicus the celestial spheres represented the working areas of spiritual beings which were then marked out by the visible planets. To this we must still add our Moon, circling around the Earth, meditating the up building stream around Full Moon phase, and the dissolving process in the New Moon phase Fig. 41. This fact was well known earlier in this century to those involved in growing plants.

Living into all these movements just described, we can feel ourselves involved in this gigantic building -up and breaking-down activity. However, we may well ask: 'Is there any purpose in these processes, or just an eternal repetition?' This is, of course, a very deep question, for it is intimately connected with the meaning of life for all humanity. Envisaging evolution as having the aim to bring something new into the Universe, our Earth is in a unique position within the process just described, enabling us to experience both the up

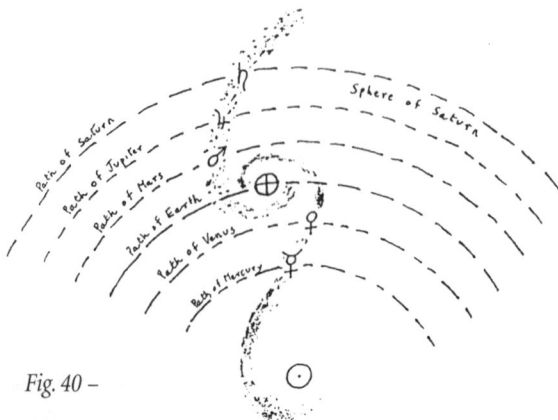

Fig. 40 –

building and the dissolving processes. When these are in the right balance, we can become conscious as human beings, and we know that this consciousness, this awareness of our surroundings, has changed in time. Going back to the height of the Persian Civilization, their leader, the great Zarathustra (c.5000 B.C.), taught his people about the God of Light, the Sun-Spirit or Ahura Mazdao who was on his way to the Earth. But, he said, the Earth was by no means ready to receive Him, and that it would need the work of mankind over a long period of time to make His coming possible. That Sun-Spirit, the Spirit of the Greater Sun, the Spirit of the whole Universe, came down to the Earth at the beginning of the era marked by the change from B.C. to A.D. For some people He is known as the Christ, but others recognise Him under different names. Like the Sun who shines on all people, this great Universal Spirit brought a new Light to Earth for the whole of humanity. However, it is within the freedom of each individual to take this gift of Light and work with it or not. Thus we can add to this picture of the Great Cosmic Sunflower, the Sun in his capacity as a fixed star, the experience of sailing through the different qualities of his twelve petals, the constellations of the Zodiac, in the course of the year.

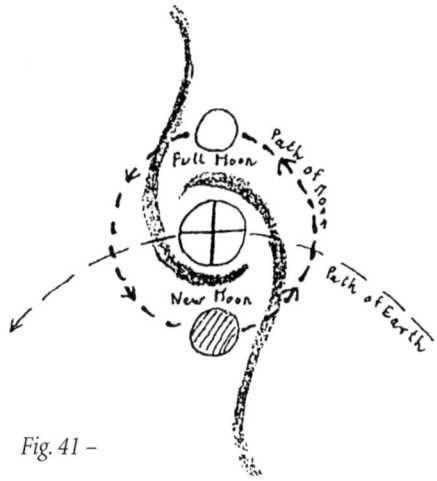

Fig. 41 –

Out of a free choice we can seek for an ever deepening understanding of these great processes so that we can take up that offering of new Light and work with it. So in the course of time we have something to ray out as a contribution towards a positive evolution of the Universe. In this way the whole of humanity is granted a share in the responsibility of evolving a 'new universe' such as is described in the Apocalypse of St. John as the New Jerusalem.

COMETS

Comet Hale-Bopp has given us a magnificent display for almost three months of this year of 1997. Few sighted people have not witnessed her and when she began to vanish from our perception many felt it as a loss of a friend. She has also awakened a great interest in and awareness of the wonders of the starry cloak enfolding our Earth. From where does a comet come and to where do they go ? Most of the rest of the starry universe visible to our unaided sight follows laws with which we can follow them and know where to look for them over long periods of time. But comets are very unpredictable and even for those whose return cycle seems to have been calculated it is never certain that they will appear at the appointed time or be as more or less visible as expected. Georg Blattmann in his book 'Comets' compares the 'biography' of a comet with that of a human being pointing out how certain facts of life are necessities but that within these there is a certain freedom. He terms them 'the Freedom Heroes of the Universe'. Rudolf Steiner in a lecture on the nature of comets (24.10.1923) said:"… if as regularly as the rising and setting of Sun and Moon, the comet with its tail were to come and again disappear, then we human beings would have no freedom; then everything else in us would be as regular as the rising and setting of the Sun and Moon".

There have been records of sightings of comets from very early in history, at least back to 240 B.C. and in Chinese historical records Halley's comet has now been traced back to 1057 B.C. This was the comet which appeared again in 1066 and is portrayed on the Bayeux Tapestry of the Battle of Hastings. In 1632 it appeared once more and Edmund Hally calculated its course to be an elongated ellipse reaching out beyond the planet paths. Having worked out that this comet would take 76 years to circuit on its path he checked earlier sightings and found many which confirmed this 76 year rhythm. He then predicted its next return to be around 1758. Hally did not live to see his prediction come true but it established the fact for other astronomers that some comets return at regular intervals which could be calculated. Since then many other comet rhythms have been discovered at varying lengths of time, the shortest being 3.3 years and a number have also been confirmed. Although there are hundreds of comet sightings most of these are only visible through a telescope. In 1950 a dutch astronomer, Jan Oort, suggested that they originate in a vast spherical cloud (the 'Oort cloud') which surrounds the solar system, far out into the universe. Some in time are drawn into the solar system and follow their elliptical paths within this system. For instance Jupiter has a 'family' of some 45 comets, whose orbital paths do not go further out than Jupiter.

Georg Blattmann in the aforementioned book has an interesting illumination of this Oort Cloud. He compares it with Raphael's Sistine Madonna which has a cloud background of many little faces of children. He suggests these are unborn souls awaiting incarnation and that it is out of this 'cloud' that Mary brings one special child into the world to carry out his earthly mission. Rudolf Steiner also speaks of each comet having its own special mission (5.3.1910).

From time to time there is expressed the fear that a meteor or comet will collide with the Earth which could bring about a major disaster. There was such a fear at the end of the last century when it was predicted that Biela's comet, with a cycle of about $6^3/_4$ of a year, would collide with the Earth at a time when it was thought the Earth would be in the point where the two orbits crossed. The calculations were then corrected and brought forward to 1933. However already in 1845 the comet was observed to have split into two, with successive appearances where the two parts had moved further apart and finally in 1872 instead of seeing the divided comet there was a spectacular rain of shooting stars. Rudolf Steiner commented on observing them as an eleven year old boy and some people thought all the stars had fallen from the sky. This was repeated a few times but with less intensity until 1933 when there was again an impressive show which since then appears as a yearly minor event of shooting stars. This seems to be the biography of many periodic comets that they gradually break up with the bits spreading out in their previous orbit which are then experienced as a rain of shooting stars when the Earth yearly crosses that path.

With all the interest aroused through the comet Hale-Bopp most of us have become familiar with the typical comet path sweeping in an elliptical curve round the Sun and passing out again through the spheres of the planets marked out by their orbits. The tail increases in brightness and length as it reaches its perihelion, the nearest point to the Sun, and according to the relative positions of Earth, Sun and comet the viewings are more or less favourable (according also to the peculiarities of the individual comets!). With Hale-Bopp this has been very favourable and in the northern hemisphere we have been graced with a magnificent spectacle over many months. The tail always appears streaming away from the Sun which the astronomers say is blown out by the 'solar wind' which radiates from the Sun, and is composed of lit up particles from the nucleus of the comet. Georg Blattmann suggests that it is a light phenomenon akin to the corona of the Sun, making that light 'visible' which is always present but otherwise only manifest when the light of the Sun is blotted out. The head of the comet travels at incredible speeds as it rounds the Sun yet the tail rays out like a searchlight and does not bend at whatever speed it travels. It is also transparent for if it passes in front of a star, however faint that star might be it does not blot it out. The tail is also known to contain traces of various elements among them iron and cyanide. Rudolf Steiner spoke of the presence of the latter in a lecture in 1906 and was very gratified when this was confirmed later by natural scientific investigation (5.3.1910). in other lectures he describes the comets as drawing impurities out of the Sun which have been amassed there, partly visible as sunspots, and dispersing them out into the universe.

This is the second year running that we have been treated with the sighting of a comet, at least those of us living in the northern hemisphere. Last year, 1996, the comet Hyakutake caught astronomers by surprise by its sudden appearance in the region of the Pole Star and passing nearer to the Earth than any comet since 1556 was expected to increase in brilliance when it passed through its perihelion nearest to the Sun. However its brilliance diminished rapidly and its visibility was of very short duration. Its calculated path, from the view-point of the Earth, moved from the region of the Virgin/Scales over the dome of the heavens, past the little Bear to Perseus and on to the Fishes bearing a very interesting relationship to the path of Hale-Bopp. These two comets illustrate the individual character of each comet. At the time of the appearance of Hyakutke astronomers were already occupied with following the path of Hale-Bopp who had already been observed through the telescopes of amatuer astronomers in 1995 far out in the sphere of Jupiter. It is interesting that most comets are discovered by amatuer astronomers, the professionals seem to focus more on one particular region of the sky.

The calculated earth-view of Hale Bopp moves from the Archer/Scorpion past Pegasus, Andromeda, Perseus and on to the Bull/Twins. Thus the two paths cross in the region of Perseus, very close to the fixed star Algol. Algol is a variable star which has a twin circulating it who diminishes its light in a rhythm of about $2\,^1/_2$ days. Last year on April 11 the comet Hyakutake was passing through this crossing point and this year also on April 11 Hale-Bopp was in this same position. It was actually possible on that night to see Algol shining through the light raying out from the nucleus of Hale-Bopp. Could these two celestial 'freedom heroes of the universe' have a message for us, appearing in this spectacular way in the last years of this century and seen by so many human beings ?

Comets have always been regarded with awe in earlier times as heralding some great event. They have been connected with souls of the dead leaving the Earth and making their way up into the heavens. Sadly some human beings followed this thought but by self termination of their god given lives when Hale-Bopp was clearly visible in the skies. Comets were also thought of as marking the birth of great souls as for instance with some artists in pictures of the birth of Jesus. As the spiritual understanding of a comet receded in the course of history they became heralds of disasters, very often of wars. It is interesting that the very spectacular appearance of comets has declined since the end of the last century. Could this be connected with the commencement of the Age of Michael in 1879? Michael who has always been associated with the Sun and with cosmic iron and who has his festival at the time of the year when there are most shooting stars to be seen in the heavens.

Let us look at some of the Greek mythological representations in the sky which are still frequently used on star maps. These mythologies came into being when spiritual insight, although fading, was still alive in at least some human beings. Therefore they are like a great picture book depicting some aspects of the development of mankind at that time with indications into the future. Willi Sucher in the first part of his book 'Isis Sophia' expresses it thus: 'We shall realise that the Greek sky was a harmonious and organic structure, revealing the ancient vision of the heavens as the coordinating link between Divine Will and human evolution'. The part of the sky which must interest us here centers around the picture of the Greek hero Perseus. Perseus is depicted flying home from a completed mission, that of overcoming the Medusa. He is represented around a certain group of stars and he holds in his hand the severed head of the Medusa which is marked by the star Algol. Medusa was one of three sister Gorgons who had been sea nymphs in the favour of Neptune. However Medusa had offended the goddess Athene who changed her into a monster with snakes instead of hair and a gaze that turned all who looked into her face to stone. Perseus was given gifts from the gods to help him overcome her: Athene her mirror-like shield, Pluto a magic helmet which made the wearer invisible and Hermes his winged sandals. Using his own wits Perseus was then able to approach Medusa backwards looking into the mirror of his shield and cut off her head. On his way back he sees Andromeda chained to a rock with a terrible sea monster approaching her to eat her up. Andromeda is the daughter of Cepheus and Cassiopea all three of whom are depicted in that area of the sky. Her mother Cassiopea, also suffered from her vanity in claiming to be more beautiful than any of the sea nymphs and rousing the wrath of Neptune who sent a sea monster to ravage the coast of Ethiopia. An oracle, when consulted, said the only way to appease the monster was for them to sacrifice their daughter Andromeda. Perseus came flying along just in time, swooping down to the monster he held the head of the Medusa in front of him and he was instantly turned to stone. One sees him in the heavens as Cetus the whale.

Perseus portrays the newly acquired faculty of reflective thinking which could overcome the old capacities of a dreamy clairvoyance that had once been good but which had then become decadent; the Medusa had been beautiful and the snake hair suggests the old symbol of wisdom, worn, for instance, on the head of the Pharaoh. This new capacity for reflective thought was manifest in the birth and development of philosophy in the Greek Age, the Age of the Ram or Aries. The constellation of Andromeda lies above the Ram and the eastern fish in the constellation of the Fishes. Andromeda, the soul of humanity, is chained to the rock of materialism which had to happen for a time as a preparation for the present age, that of the consciousness soul.

The movements, gestures and relationships within the starry world which once manifested the direct workings of Divine spiritual beings have now become expressions of their 'wrought or accomplished work' (see Letter VI in The Michael Mystery by Rudolf Steiner). For the gods no longer guide us as little children but stand back to let us develop our adulthood waiting expectantly to receive fruits from our earth lives as spiritual substance for the future. Perseus was directly aided by the gods but

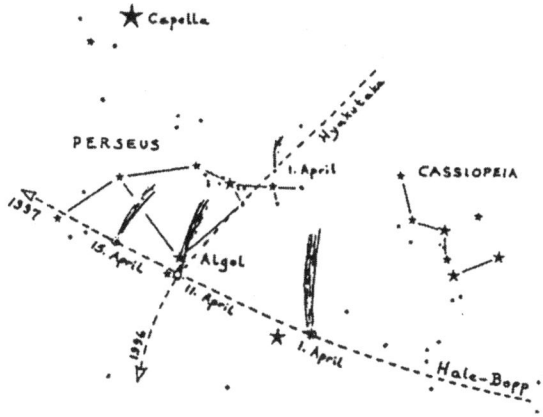

Fig. 42 –

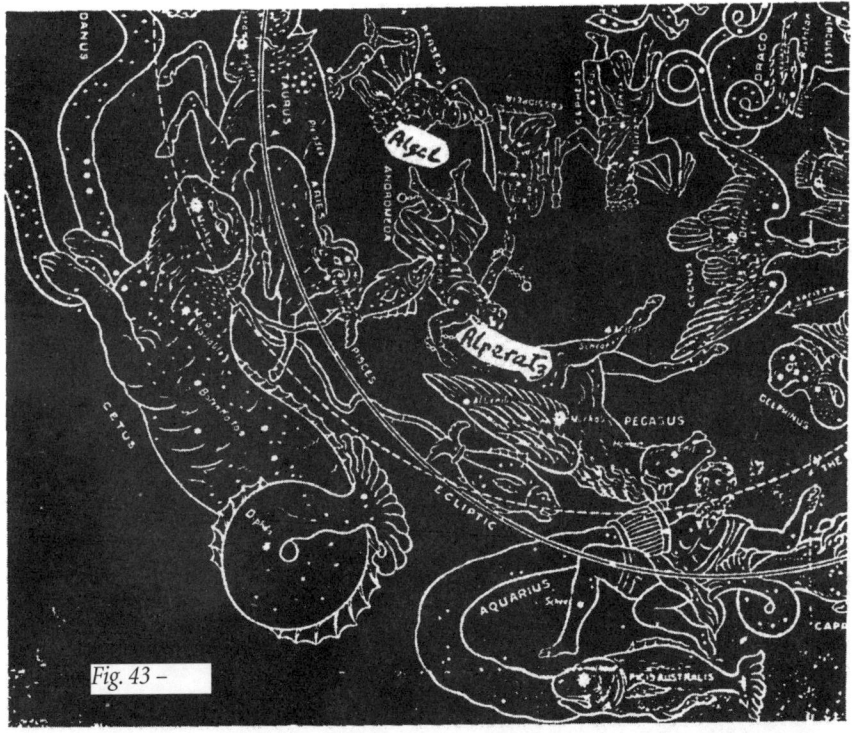

Fig. 43 –

we now have these gifts within us as sleeping capacities waiting to be awakened. The faculty to do this is hidden in the myth we have been considering. It is recounted that from the drops of blood falling from the severed head of the Medusa sprang the winged horse Pegasus, who is represented by a group of stars next to Andromeda. Alpharatz, the star on Andromeda's forehead is shared by the constellation of Pegasus who flies above the western one of the two Fishes and Aquarius. The Vernal Point is at present below that western Fish, gradually moving towards Aquarius, already announcing the coming Age of the Waterman or Aquarius. Rudolf Steiner, referring to the movement of the Vernal Point, said: 'Now the Sun has been in the sign of the Fishes for several centuries. In the near future it will have advanced so far in this sign that it will be the outer symbol for the appearance of Christ in the etheric body' (18.4.1910.)

Once and once only did Christ appear in the physical realm, 2000 years ago which culminated in His great Deed on Golgotha. His second appearance in this century was a Deed performed in the etheric realm, that realm veiled to our ordinary senses but manifesting in the mysteries of life and perceptible to spirit vision ('winged intelligence'?). The horse in mythology is connected with intelligence and here Pegasus bears wings. Speaking of this second coming of Christ in the etheric Rudolf Steiner said: 'The event to which we refer is that human beings can acquire the new faculty of perception in the etheric realm' (25.1.1910).

Could these two 'freedom heroes of the universe' be awaiting fruits from the further development of our consciousness to the experience of this second great Deed of Christ that we can live and work out of His Presence in the etheric realm?

The Stars spake once to Man.	*But in the deepening silence*
It is World destiny	*There grows and ripens*
That they are silent now.	*What Man speaks to the Stars.*
To be aware of that silence	*To be aware of that speaking*
Can be pain for earthly Man.	*Can become strength for Spirit Man.*

References:

Sternkalender   Ostern 1997 - Ostern 1998 Mathematisch - Astronomischen Sektion am Goetheanum Dornach Schweiz

Atlas of the Solar System David A. Hardy, Peerage Books London

The Mysterious Universe Nigel Henbest, Ebury Press London

Some Thoughts on the Christian Festivals and their Celebration in Different Regions of the Earth.

For most people the Sun gives us our daily and yearly rhythms in life. He is a living being and cannot be squeezed into dead, mechanical or abstract forms as we use in our timepieces and calendars. Therefore we have to introduce Greenwich 'Mean' Time (G.M.T.) and 'leap' years to conform as nearly as possible with the living rhythm of the Sun. Within our yearly calendar certain dates have been allied to various festivals and among them are the Christian Festivals of Christmas, St Johns', and Michaelmas. Easter, a very main Christian Festival is an exception and is still determined yearly by the relationship of the Sun, Moon and the Earth. It commemorates the Deed of Christ which took place in the northern hemisphere on the first Sunday after the Full Moon following the Sun's passage across the equinox point in the Spring season of his yearly path. Thus the Sun was ascending out of the dark days of winter, the Moon was on the wane and then it was the first Sun-day on the Earth. This was the culmination of a process which we can follow from the Birth of Jesus, through the following thirty and three years to the uniting of the Christ Being with the Earth at the first Easter: The seed for a new reunion of the Heavens and the Earth when the rhythms of these two need to be in a particular relationship. The all important Ascension and Whitsun Event experienced by the Apostles, and others in varying degrees, is celebrated 40 and 50 days after Easter. These four main Christian Festival times are very close to the pre-christian seasonal ones for the equinox and solstice times of the year. One could perhaps say that these earlier celebrations were taken up by the Christ and after a pause of a few days reinstituted in a new way. Thus in the northern hemisphere we have retained much of the seasonal, nature element in our traditional celebrations. In fact the 'seasonal' colouring has very much overshadowed the deeper Christian understanding of the festival in the outer forms of the celebration.

Thus it has become a big question for those living in the southern hemisphere (also for those dwelling in the so-called tropical zones) for instance, how to celebrate the 'winter' mood of Christmas in the heat of midsummer. I experienced preparations for Christmas in Australia with the stores decorated with 'snow' covered Christmas trees and Santa's sledge, supported by traditional carols loudly proclaiming winter scenes. However it has challenged many people to seek an understanding of the events which took place 2000 years ago and what they mean to us today right down into our daily life. The question also comes up: Is it important for a world wide humanity to celebrate together or is it more important to relate to the outer events in nature, especially in connection with the cycle of the year? Regions on the Earth where the seasons can be defined as Spring, Summer, Autumn (Fall) and Winter lie within a small range of latitudes in the northern and southern hemisphere, the changes being more pronounced in the northern half. Even in regions where typical seasons have been experienced there are increasingly wide variations in the weather both daily and weekly which can be likened to the whole cycle of the year. Altogether our Earth appears as a threefold being with a tropical zone between north and south, where the course of the year manifests in a very different form.

There is one unifying factor in all this for the Sun and the planets shine down on the whole Earth in their manifold relationship to the Zodiac. If we could see the visible starry constellation behind the Sun we would find it is the same all over the world. In our age, for all places on which the Sun shines during the Christmas season he rays down to us from the direction of the Archer or Sagittarius; likewise from the Twins or Gemini on St Johns' Day, and the Virgin or Virgo at Michaelmas. How conscious are most of us of a changing quality of sunlight as the Sun passes before the twelve constellations of the Zodiac in the course of the year? A quality apart from the seasonal one.

In 1911 Imma von Eckardstein, a close associate of Rudolf Steiner asked him for some help in experiencing the course of the year. Besides giving her the 52 mantric verses coming out of the soul moods and challenges during the year he gave her the task of working at a new mythology of the constellations of the Zodiac. She was to take the whole 'mood' while observing the Sun rising in front of the twelve different constellations of the Zodiac and let it resound in her soul until there arose imaginative experiences. Working together with Dr Steiner and these practical exercises there came into being the twelve motives as the seed form of a new mythology which were reproduced in the Soul Calendar of 1912/13. This original calendar was a threefold creation containing also a large number of dates concerning historic personalities and events. The motives were not able to be reproduced in colour, which belonged to the expression of the Imagination, and for various reasons have never been included in reprints of the 52 verses. Dr Steiner had hoped that a group of artists would work further on these 'seed' motives, however very few individuals are known to have taken up this work. Suso Vetter mentions some in an extensive supplement on the Soul Calendar to the 1989/90 Sternkalendar[1].

In 1935 Margot Roessler[2] made this her life task and gave many lectures and workshops also on new motives for the seven planets and the Earth. Imma von Eckardstein had also initiated this work on the planets during the life time of Rudolf Steiner.

This was one way of looking through the outer sense impressions to the reality of the spiritual out of which they were brought to birth. The realm of the stars and in particular the Zodiac has always been regarded in the mystery schools as a great book spread out around us in which the story of creation could be found by those who could read it. The new Zodiac representations are also expressions of stages of Evolution.

The fact that through the ages the Sun, at the time of the Christian Festivals changes his message, through the precession of the equinox, from one group of Beings to another can help substantiate the fact that through the evolution of consciousness we are able to evolve our understanding of the particular festival we are seeking to celebrate. For instance, the date given for the birth of Jesus from which has evolved our Christmas Festival was at a time when the Sun shone down from the constellation of the Goat or Capricorn whereas in our time, as we said earlier, we experience the stars of the Archer or Sagittarius behind the Christmas Sun. Many wonderful events have happened during those 2000 years including a further Deed of the Christ Being in the 20th century which would challenge us to wake up to an ever deeper relationship to that 'birth process'. Many people have experienced this as giving real substance to their lives.

Through the Deed of Christ in the 20th century we are able to grow ever more conscious of what weaves behind the sense experiences in nature and this we need to cultivate in order to gain a deeper understanding of that mysterious realm of life. It becomes increasingly important because we have been granted the power to meddle in this realm without being aware of the dire consequences of our experiments, often promoted by the feeling of power, curiosity, or just plain fascination. Here we come back to the cycle of the year in nature which we have noted is in the first place a regional experience. Can we find a meaningful relationship to a Christian Festival and the regional experience of the Earth's environment in any one place?

Maybe we must make our thoughts and experiences more mobile. Dr Steiner gives a wonderfully alive imagination of the four Archangels who have always been connected with the four seasons [3]. He describes how they constantly work, circling around the whole Earth, now raying down from the heights through nature to us and the opposite time of the year raying up through the Earth into our inner nature. Working in pairs Gabriel shines down from above over the Christmas time in the northern hemisphere while Uriel works from below, through the Earth from where it is then midsummer. Thus if we can become aware of how we are part of this weaving together of Uriel, Gabriel, Raphael and Michael then the course of the year can be lifted up to an Earth-wide experience as well as a regional one.

In his book 'Cosmic Christianity' where Willi Sucher speaks of the Sun in relationship to the Three Years of Christ's Ministry on Earth he pictures three Zodiacs. The one furthest away from the Earth manifests in the world of the visible fixed stars, the Zodiac and all the other groups of stars. Coming nearer to the Earth we come to the path of the Sun in the course of the year, the ecliptic. From our viewpoint on the Earth we experience the Sun marking out our calendar year as he passes before the twelve visible constellations of the Zodiac but also through the Zodiac of the twelve divisions of the ecliptic. (See Willi Sucher's 'Isis Sophia – Introducing Astrosophy', Second Letter.) This (apparent) path of the Sun is a mathematical reality only discernible through outer facts. For instance, the world wide experience of equal day and night at the equinox times when the Sun rises due east and sets due west. Or when the longest or shortest day with the Sun at his highest or lowest point at midday at solstice times manifests as the opposite in the two hemispheres. This seems to be directly connected with the seasons, nature, the realm of life or etheric in the Earth.

The third Zodiac comes about through our orientation to space from any one point on Earth. These are the so-called 'houses' and are described by Willi Sucher as being like 'twelve receptacles that relate cosmic facts to Earth reality'. It is as if we look out through twelve windows around us, six below the horizon and six above and 'observe' the stars as we turn on our Earth from sunrise to sunrise. Our windows lie on the south-north axis of a given location like the segments of a 'space-orange'. These three Zodiacs could be tentatively thought of as manifesting the astral, etheric and physical body of the cosmos. (See Willi Sucher, 'Cosmic Christianity'.)

Let us turn our thoughts towards the coming into being of our Christian Festivals, especially to the time when Christ walked our Earth in the bodily vessel of Jesus. From the time of the Baptism in the Jordan the 'cosmic individuality of the Christ' worked through that bodily vessel of Jesus. Because of the very special preparation of that body 'the forces active within Him were the cosmic forces from the Sun and the Stars; and these directed His body'[4]. If we picture the greater Being of the Cosmic Christ reaching up to encompass the starry heavens and beyond it is obvious that the Deeds which He carried out on Earth would be in harmony with the whole Universe. From these Deeds flowed spiritual nourishment to all the hierarchical beings within that Universe which laid the seed for its eventual transubstantiation. The life of Christ on Earth was an archetypal act presented in freedom, to invite mankind to partake and become gardeners of those seeds so that they can grow, mature and produce Fruit. Christ came to Earth, united Himself with her that His divine forces could then stream through the whole Earth and inaugurate a new era of the working together of the Gods and Mankind. The consciousness of mankind has evolved since then and following a further Deed of Christ in the 20th century we can choose to take an ever fuller part in this great work of transformation.

Spiritual Beings have sacrificed their forward evolution to create this world of materially visible objects in which we live that we could develop self awareness. Having learnt much in this direction it now behoves us to sharpen our awareness of the spiritual realities shining through our fellow human beings and the visible world around us, right out to the stars. In as much as we can do this the veil of the sense perceptible world falls away releasing spiritual beings to continue their arrested evolutionary process. This is the process which Rudolf Steiner calls 'speaking to the Stars' in a verse describing the changing relationship of mankind to the stars, picturing the stars here as manifestations of spiritual beings [5].

To take up this responsibility can now shine through how we celebrate our festivals but the query still remains of how to celebrate them in the various regions of the Earth. This is a comparatively recent question which stems from the spread of Christianity to the southern regions of the Earth and the evolution of our consciousness which rightly demands that we live no more with mere traditions but learn to know how we conduct our lives.

Could we try to look at this question from a contemplation of the three Zodiacs? Starting from the universal aspect of the fixed star world we would be in a region of awareness which is not limited by temporal considerations but directly in the flow of true spiritual realities, that world from which the Christ comes and which is our true home. From this aspect it would seem to me that we would need to offer up our human contribution all together from all parts of the world. It would be illumined by the common experience of the Sun 'rising' in a particular constellation as a 'symbol' of our Ego or 'I' consciousness and enriched by the planets in their relationship to the fixed star Zodiac and to each other at that chosen time. This would give the inspiration for a unique offering each year.

Then, we could begin to add the next level of awareness to our contribution, that of the Christ-filled, living cycle of the year, the regional nature processes within the breathing of the Earth. Here we could briefly consider the uniqueness within the relationship of the two hemispheres. The proportions of land and ocean are very different; the north pole area is exclusively frozen water whereas at the south pole there is much solid land. However, otherwise the land masses in the south are much smaller than those in the north and tapering in shape with a preponderance of the watery element. The vegetation, animals and insect life are also very different. Thinking of the large amount of ocean in the south could lead to the thought of a 'reflective' relationship to the northern hemisphere. Adding this to the picture of the encircling archangels could perhaps help one to understand how it is that the Sun shining from the Ram sector of the ecliptic seems to call forth Spring in the northern hemisphere when at the same time it is Autumn on the other half of the Earth. The mystery of the interweaving of beings across the circle of the Zodiac surely also plays a large part. Rudolf Steiner refers to the new pictures of the Zodiac constellations as 'representations of actual experiences connected with the waking and sleeping of particular Spiritual Beings'[6].

And the third Zodiac of the 'Twelve receptacles'? Could we look at this in the light of the individual human beings, as receptacles of the Christ Spirit, amongst whom we carry out our celebration even if it is only one, ourselves?

I would like to close these considerations with a verse from the first part of Goethe's Faust:

Into the Whole how all things weave,

One in another work and live!
What heavenly forces up and down are ranging,
The golden buckets interchanging,
With wafted benison winging,
From Heaven through the Earth are springing,
All through the All harmonious ringing!

1. *Tierkreis Imaginationen und Gedenktage im Jahreslauf - Beilage zum Sternkalender Ostern 1998* - Ostern 1990 Goetheanum, Dornach. German only
2. *From the Language of the Zodiac I, The Sun-Zodiac experience.* The only work of Margot Roessler available in English. From Botton Bookshop, U.K.
3. *The Four Seasons and the Archangels*, Lecture 5. Rudolf Steiner, 13.10.1923.
4. *Spiritual Guidance of Man*, Lecture III. Rudolf Steiner, 8.6.1911.
5. *'Stars spake once to Man'* Verses and Meditations, Rudolf Steiner
6. *Calendar of the Soul*, Lecture 7.5.1912. Rudolf Steiner.

The Bio-Dynamic Impulse and Star Challenges at the Turn of the Millennium

The Bio-Dynamic Impulse was born at Koberwitz in 1924 when Dr. Steiner celebrated a Whitsun Festival with about 130 people who took part in his lectures, later to be known as the Agricultural Course. This event has been wonderfully remembered in written pictures put together by Adalbert Graf von Keyserlink in a book titled 'Koberwitz' 1924, published in Germany in 1974. Sadly this book has not been available to English readers. However there are great hopes that by Easter 1999 it will be published in an English translation†. John Wood, a great friend of the Bio-Dynamic Impulse had just completed a translation of it before crossing over the threshold on September 22 of this year. We owe him deep gratitude for completing this important task before moving on to other realms of activity. That gathering in Koberwitz was a truly Whitsun Event and that it should come again to our notice is in keeping with the challenges of this last year of the century. The magnitude of the deed of Rudolf Steiner has given us a unique and vital tool with which to counter the thoughtless ravages of our Earth, in all four kingdoms of Earth, Plant, Animal and Man. Apart from all the practical advice given the crowning has been the Preparations through which we can work at maintaining the link with the formative forces from the heavens from which we are in danger of being severed.

In the book referred to Johanna Graf von Keyserlingk writes about an esoteric hour which Rudolf Steiner held on the Whitsunday after they had all been on a land walk through the estate. There Dr. Steiner stressed the importance of the meditative life for the land worker and how through that one could connect with spiritual beings and enlist their help to work down in a healing way into the whole environment of the farm community and the life of the plants. He then nodded towards Dr. Vreede, to whom he had given the task to lead the Mathematical-Astronomical Section in Dornach, and said that through her work the connecting with the Spirits of the Spheres could be attained. And then through the whole course he was constantly referring especially to the planets and their connection with the earthly realm in a detailed way. This New Star Wisdom which Dr. Vreede pioneered and which has become known as Astrosophy (her suggestion) strives to reach out to the spiritual beings manifesting through the starry world in a fully conscious way, being aware that they are waiting in confident expectation for us to bring them fruits of our life experiences on Earth. Can we find any relationship between some starry events at this turning point of the millennium and the Whitsun Deed of 1924 ?

On May 28 and June 11 of the year 2000 two special star events take place which sound out the same challenge to mankind. Willi Sucher, who took up Dr. Vreede's

---

† *Now available. 'The Birth of a New Agriculture Koberwitz 1924' edited by Adalbert Graf von Keyserling – Temple Lodge, London ISBN 1-902636-07-4.*

impulse and worked for many years on the seed beginnings of Astrosophy, had a deep concern for humanity, increasingly so towards the end of his life in 1985. It was born out of living with that event of May 28, 2000 which will be a so-called Great Conjunction, a meeting between the planets Saturn and Jupiter.(Fig.44) They come together in a rhythm of about 20 years but in three different directions of the Zodiac. Thus they meet in the same constellation about every 60 years. This great 'triangle' rotates very slowly within the Zodiac and so one can follow a particular conjunction back, or forward in time. Willi Sucher has carried out a deep research into the rhythms and gestures of the planets during the Three Years of Christ's Ministry on Earth and their subsequent rhythmic repetitions, which are never exactly the same. This special moment at the 'turning point of time' Christ walked the Earth and was at the same time in harmony with all the spiritual hierarchies manifesting through the stars, which were an integral part of His greater Being. An archetypal picture of what we have the potential to rise to in the future. A 'conversation' where His spiritual deeds on Earth imbued the starry beings with a renewing substance. This then is carried through time silently offering challenges to mankind each time the gestures recur, waiting for a response from human beings. Following this point of the triangle back to the time of Christ on Earth we find a similar conjunction taking place in the year after the Mystery of Golgotha, 34 AD. This is the year when the event recorded in the 9th chapter of the Acts

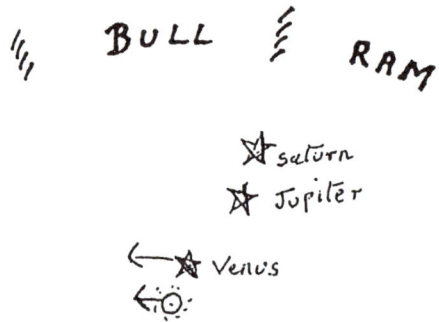

Fig. 44–
May 28, 2000 and
movement of Sun and
Venus to June 11 2000

of the Apostles is reckoned to have taken place, the experience of Saul at the Gate of Damascus and his subsequent transformation into Paul for whom the Resurrected Christ was a constant, living reality. He was the first human being who had not recognised the Christ as He walked on Earth to experience the Risen Christ within, 'yet not I, but the grace of God which was with me' (I Corinthians 15:10). This was granted to the Apostles at the first Whitsun Event and since the second Deed of Christ in the first third of this century is increasingly possible for every human being during the next 2,500 years.

On Whitsunday of the year 2000, June 11, Venus and the Sun will meet in a superior conjunction with Venus beyond the Sun as seen from the Earth. These two planets meet about every 10 months and in five different directions of the Zodiac. Venus is alternately beyond the Sun and between the Sun and Earth. Thus in about eight years she has five inner or inferior conjunctions and five superior ones. If we join these meeting points we can arrive at a double five-pointed 'star'. This invisible but mathematically real star rotates very slowly within the Zodiac in a similar way to the 'triangle' of the Saturn-Jupiter conjunctions. Thus one can also follow the points of this star back or forward in time. There were only three conjunctions during the Three Years of Christ dwelling in the vessel of Jesus but one just before the Baptism and one the year fol-

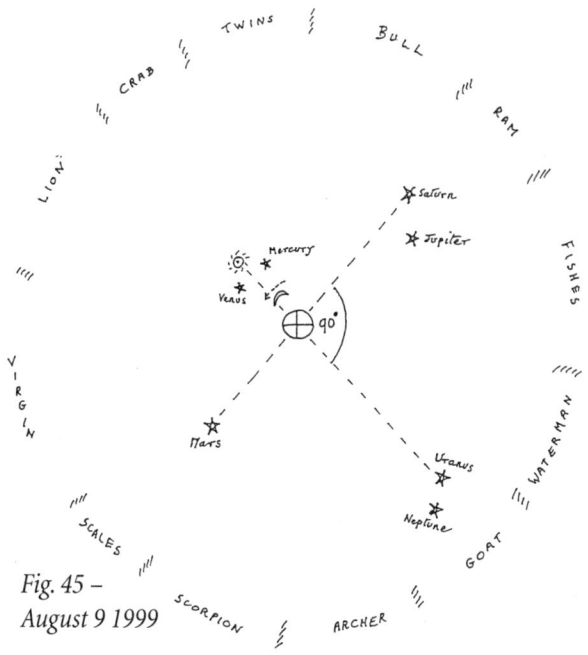

Fig. 45 –
August 9 1999

lowing the Golgotha Events. Two were inferior and three superior. Following these gestures up Willi Sucher experienced them as taking up five Deeds especially connected with the renewal of the Mysteries many of which had become decadent at that time or in need of new Life. Further information on this subject can be found in Willi Sucher's book 'Cosmic Christianity and the Changing Countenance of Cosmology. The conjunction we are considering in 2000 can be followed back to the year 34AD and again bears the living memory of the Saul/Paul experience. Since the year 1997 we have been living with the challenges of this sequence of events nearly 2000 years ago. The first three have sounded out and the fourth, questioning us about the Raising of Lazarus and the events of Easter Week 33AD, will take place on August 20, 1999. Thus in the early part of the year 2000 there will be a double sounding of the challenge - 'What do you human beings understand of the Saul/Paul Event; will you live on into the new millennium as Saul or Paul ?'

Following back that point of the Venus pentagonal 'star' to 1924 we come to an inferior conjunction between the Sun and Venus on July 1. This is about two weeks after the Whitsun celebration at the birth of the Bio-Dynamic Impulse but already on June 10. Venus started her retrograde movement to go back and let the slower moving Sun catch her up. The strongest challenge can often come before or after the actual conjunction. Thus this deed of Rudolf Steiner together with all the strivings which many human beings have offered up while working with this Impulse will sound out on the Paul side of the great question put to mankind in the year 2000.

Another striking starry configuration will occur in August 1999 Fig. 45. Between August 7 and 11 there will be exact square or 90° aspects between the planets Sun, Mars, Uranus and Saturn. Jupiter is not far from Saturn, the Sun is flanked by Mercury and Venus and Neptune 12° behind Uranus. The Moon passes Mercury and is opposite Neptune on the 10th and the following day moves across the face of the Sun giving a total eclipse (visible as total in the U.K. only as far north as Cornwall) and passing opposite to Uranus. On the 12th she passes Venus. A great 'square' like this one was considered a very bad omen by some but Dr. Steiner has given us a wonderful example as to how to reply to such a challenge. When he was giving a course of lectures in Stockholm on the Gospel of St John in relation to the other Gospels, (in January 1910)he was asked by one of the members not to give a lecture on a day when the 'square aspects were supposed to be especially powerful'. Dr. Steiner said: 'Tell the members the lecture will take place' and it was then that he spoke for the first time about the Etheric Christ Event. First to a small group in the form of an esoteric lesson of which there are no notes but then in a lecture to all the members. Following this example we could perhaps suggest the following response to this question posed by the starry beings in August 1999. During these days from August 7-11 the Sun moves from the constellation of the Crab into that of the Lion. The events are considered as related to an unequal division of the constellations of the Zodiac. (Other views are now expressed in this matter but the universe is too great to be comprehended from one point of view alone.) Thinking now of the beings of the Saturn sphere who are the faithful recorders of all that comes to pass we return to the time of the Mystery of Golgotha. Saturn was then passing through the constellation of the Crab or Cancer but by the first Whitsun he had just entered the region of the Lion. Could this then prompt us to find a response to the situation in August 1999 out of the sequence of Events between Golgotha and Whitsun so graphically described by Rudolf Steiner in the 'Fifth Gospel'? This is just a brief suggestion which could be furthered by a consideration of the beings manifesting through the constellations involved and working through the spheres of the planets.

A further consideration was pointed out by a conjunction between Mars and the Sun on May 12, 1998 which took place in almost exactly the same direction in the Zodiac as Saturn and Jupiter will meet on May 28, 2000. From the Heliocentric or Sun centered view of the universe this is the direction of the node of Mars. These nodes are the crossing places of the orbits of the planets which are set at slightly different levels of obliquity to each other. Rudolf Steiner calls them Gateways between the different spheres. The first half of the Earth evolution is known as the Mars half. The beings working out of the Mars sphere had the task of forming for us a solid Earth with all its implications. Death as a finality came for mankind as a consequence of this hardening, materialising activity. However the Deed of Christ broke through this veil which endangered human beings and the Earth of being totally separated from the spiritual realities. War and conflict had their role to play and in this the Mars beings were very active. However with the Deed of Christ on Golgotha the mission of the second half of the Earth evolution was to become Mercurial. In a lecture given in Neuch tel on December 18, 1912 Rudolf Steiner Recounts how the Mars beings were unable of themselves to transform their activities to meet the new requirements. He tells how by the year 1600 the Mars culture needed to receive an upward impulse and how 'the Earth was the only place where one could know what the situation on Mars was like'. So already then mankind had become responsible for the welfare of other spiritual beings! We can be grateful to Christian Rosenkreutz that he was awake to the situation and sent 'his closest friend and pupil', the Gautama Buddha, to Mars who performed for Mars a deed similar to what the Mystery of Golgotha was for the Earth. We all pass through the Mars sphere between death and rebirth and through the Rosicrucian path can also reach out in meditation while dwelling on the Earth to partake in this great procesd of transforma-

tion, for the soul of Gautama Buddha 'is utterly dedicated to the work of the Christ Impulse'. Thus this vast background which we have only been able to just indicate shines also through the great challenges at the turn of the millennium.

To mention one final contribution to this complex of events we turn to a visible one taking place on February 23, 1999 Fig.46. Over the Christmas Days and through January Venus has been visible as evening star shortly after sundown. Jupiter, gradually drawing

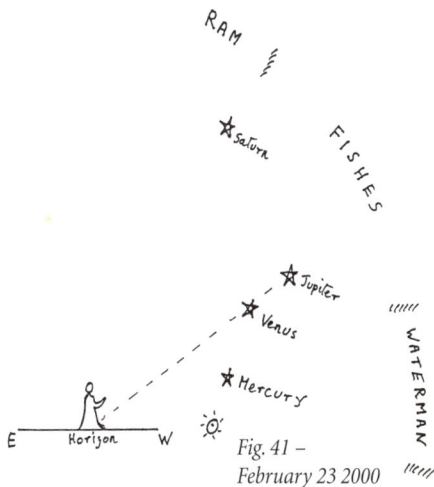

Fig. 41 –
February 23 2000

near Saturn has accompanied us in the night sky for many months. Now Venus can be seen approaching closer and closer to Jupiter whom she will catch up exactly at 19.48 GMT about the time when both planets set in the west (as viewed from mid Europe and the U.K.). The exceptional thing about this meeting is the nearness of the two planets, they will be only 0 07` apart. The last time they met was on April 22 1998 they were 0°15' apart. These are the two brightest planets and it should be quite a show for those able to view it when they will almost appear to become one brilliant star flanked by Saturn above and Mercury, who has just appeared as evening star, closer to the western horizon. John Meeks writes of this event in the Dornach Sternkalender and refers to an even closer conjunction of Jupiter and Venus in 2 BC. From Palestine they would have been seen to merge to one bright point just before setting in the west. The Great Conjunction of 7BC has been thought by some to have been the 'Star of the Three Kings' which announced to them the birth of the child. However John Meeks and others suggest that 'Star' was perhaps a whole complex of events in the heavens and might this merging of Jupiter and Venus not have been one of them ? Is this maybe another indication that 'the Time is at Hand' ?

Remarkable events are happening increasingly in the world, both positive and negative. The negative, Saul ones hit the headlines but many positive, Paul events are manifesting qualities in human beings which have never appeared before to the same extent. Perhaps the two most noticeable are the power of true forgiveness and the recognition that conflicts can only be solved through the meeting of one human being with another. Recognising and helping to bring to birth the Spirit in every human being.

In view of a specific increasing challenge I should like to add the following to this report. Genetic Engineering is directed to the very force or basis of Life. We need to muster all our strength, meditative and outer, to counter this attack. We need to enlist the help of those Spiritual Beings as reported by Johanna Graef von Keyserlingh not only to protect our environment but also to help us make real the Pauline experience - of that Greater Being, the Bestower of Life, the Risen Christ.